BAD STUFF

IN THE

NEWS

A Guide to Handling the Headlines

Rabbi Marc Gellman AND
Monsignor Thomas Hartman

SEASTAR BOOKS • NEW YORK

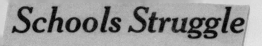

Schools Struggle

SeaStar Books
A division of North-South Books Inc.

First published in hardcover in the United States in 2002 by SeaStar Books, a division of North-South Books Inc., New York. Published simultaneously in Canada by North-South Books, an imprint of Nord-Süd Verlag AG, Gossau Zürich, Switzerland. First SeaStar Books paperback edition published in 2003.

Library of Congress Cataloging-in-Publication Data
Gellman, Marc
Bad stuff in the news: a guide to handling the headlines / by Marc Gellman and Thomas Hartman.
    p. cm.
Summary: Discusses how such problems as terrorism, child abuse, natural disasters, violence in sports, and hate crimes are reported in the media and some things that individuals can do to address the problems.
1. Mass media and children—Juvenile literature. 2. Television and children—Juvenile literature.
3. Television and broadcasting of news—Psychological aspects—Juvenile literature. [1. Social problems in mass media. 2. Violence in mass media. 3. Mass media—Influence.] I. Hartman, Thomas. II. Title.
HQ784.M3 G45 2002
302.23—dc21

Book design by Meredith Pratt
Cover photograph by Stephen de las Heras
Cover design by Matthew Siee

ISBN 1-58717-132-5 (reinforced trade edition)
RTE 10 9 8 7 6 5 4 3 2 1
ISBN 1-58717-232-1 (paperback edition)
PB 10 9 8 7 6 5 4 3 2 1

Printed in U.S.A.

For more information about our books, and the authors and artists who create them, visit our web site: www.northsouth.com

To all of the people who are fixing the bad stuff in the news today so that tomorrow, only the good stuff will be left.

7. THE HATE THAT LEADS TO HARM — 65

When you see people hurt others because of the color of their skin or their religion or where they're from . . . when people hate governments so much that they blow up buildings . . . when hate is so strong, it leads people to kill.

8. REALLY BAD SPORTS — 73

When you go to see a good game but end up seeing a bad fight . . . when people play to hurt and not for the love of the game . . . when parents don't play by the rules of sportsmanship . . . when sports are dangerous and not fun.

9. MUCKING UP THE EARTH — 81

When dead fish float down a polluted river . . . when you see oil-covered birds and otters after an oil spill . . . when food you think is safe is a poison . . . when clean air and clean water and clean dirt are hard to find . . . when people mess with the environment.

10. SAD & SCARY ADDICTS — 89

When you see famous people ruined by drugs . . . when you see ordinary people killed by drunk drivers . . . when drug dealers shoot people and get shot . . . when people think that they need chemicals to be happy.

11. SICK, DYING PEOPLE — 99

When little babies who didn't do anything to anybody get sick and die . . . when diseases spread all over the world and kill millions of people . . . when old people forget who they are . . . when people have to fight their bodies to live.

12. BAD FOR THEM, GOOD FOR YOU? — 109

When you see stuff on TV that upsets other people, but not you . . . when your clothes or music freak out your parents . . . when the bad stuff doesn't seem so bad to you.

13. LIFE ISN'T PERFECT YET — 115

When you finally understand that life isn't perfect and that this is perfectly okay.

INTRODUCTION

Has this happened to you? Because this has happened to us a lot: You turn on the television to watch the news because you want to find out if your team won. You're tired from school and tired of listening to your parents yakking at you about doing this and not doing that. It's not that you *don't* want to know what is going on in the world, it's just that you'd mostly like to hear the sports report—and maybe also get a little look at how the people on planet earth are doing today. So what happens when the news comes on?

First the news guy or the news gal smiles at the camera and says a cheerful hello. (This is the last cheerful thing you're likely to see on the news.) Then, the first story is always something horrible. Maybe it's full of awful pictures like those scenes of planes crashing into the World Trade Center or the tall buildings burning and falling to the ground. Maybe it's a story about some kid who brought guns to school and shot a bunch of people for no reason, and you see kids screaming and crying, police running with their guns drawn, and a bunch of parents absolutely freaked out. Or maybe the news is about some plane crash or flood or earthquake, and you see bodies being dug out from under piles of rubble. Or maybe you see starving kids with sunken eyes who may already be dead by now. Or maybe you see war, murder, terrorist bombings, gang violence, or drug dealers who just shot some police. Or maybe that night the news person is telling you about all of the pollution in your food, and you discover that everything you love to eat is so filled with poison and crud that you might just as well suck up some sewer water.

All this time you're getting more and more bummed out by all of the bad stuff in the news . . . and you probably get so depressed or scared that you turn off the set and you never do find out if your team won. This may never have happened to you, but it happens to us a lot.

This book is supposed to help you deal with all of this bad stuff in the news. (Finding out if your team won is *your* job.) What we worry about is that the bad stuff in the news might do some bad stuff to you:

We worry that the bad stuff in the news might make you afraid. After seeing a big office building crash to the ground, you might worry that your parents aren't safe at work. After seeing kids shooting other kids at school, you might wonder if you could get shot at your school. You might think that the world is so scary that the only safe place is hiding under your bed. We want you to understand the real dangers in the world, but we also want you to be brave and hopeful. Even though bad stuff happens sometimes, you have to find some way to feel safe and live your life without fear.

We also worry that you might start to believe that bad stuff is normal stuff. You might think that nobody can make a difference and that there's no way to fix any of the broken parts of the world. This attitude is called cynicism and we don't want you to become a cynic. It's hard to see suffering children, homeless people, and sick people night after night and still care about them. Bad stuff can form a kind of crust over your feelings. You can forget what it's like to need help. One of the main reasons we wrote this book is to help you stay soft and caring in a world that sometimes tries to turn you into someone who is hard and uncaring.

Seeing too much bad stuff can make you even more than uncaring. It might even make you forget the difference between right and wrong. The fact that there are creeps in the world who have no idea that hurting or killing is wrong doesn't mean that you have to fall to their level. You can make good choices even when other people in the world are making bad ones. So learning about what happens when bad choices are made can actually help you learn to make good ones.

You can make good choices even when other people in the world are making bad ones.

Another thing we worry about is that becoming hardened to the bad stuff in the news might cause you to lose your anger. Most of the people who have made a big difference in the world have done it by being really angry about the bad stuff in the world. It's hard to fix the world if you're not really angry about injustice and cruelty and oppression and slavery and hatred and poverty and illness. Anger isn't hatred. Hatred hurts you inside, but anger can be the fuel that gives you the strength to change what needs to be changed in the world.

If you believe that God is good and smart and powerful, it's hard to figure out why there's so much bad stuff in the world God created. Some people say that the reason there's bad stuff is that there's no God. But we believe that God exists and that God made the world with holes in it so that we could fill up the holes ourselves and have something important to do with our lives. And a lot of the bad stuff isn't God's fault at all, but *our* fault for making bad choices.

We are a rabbi and a priest and so we believe that faith in God helps people get through the bad stuff; there's a way to keep your faith *and* watch the news—lots of people do it every day. Well, we know there are at least two of them, and if you keep believing in God despite all the bad stuff in the news, you could be at least number three!

If this bad stuff is so bad, do you ever wonder why the TV, newspaper, and magazine newspeople put so much bad news on the air for us to see or on the page for us to read? There's a saying in the news business: "If it bleeds, it leads." In other words, the most bloody and terrible stories usually get the most space in the news.

Even though people say they're disgusted by all the bloody stories, secretly they really like to watch the bloody stories. People slow down when they pass accidents on the other side of the road. Some people go to car races and hockey games not to see a good race or a good game but to see crashes, fighting, and blood. There's something deep inside us that's drawn to bad stuff the way flies are drawn to poop.

Maybe the thing in us that likes bloody news is the part that's saying, "Boy, am I glad that didn't happen to me!" We like to be reminded that we are alive and well, even if that means hearing that others are hurting more than we are. Or maybe the reason is that there are so many news shows and so many papers and magazines that the people who make them are worried that nobody is going to watch or read them. They figure if they put on bad, bloody, horrible news, they can grab more viewers or readers, which means they can sell their commercials for more money (which means that they'll get to keep their jobs and their cars and the credit cards that let them eat lunch for free).

One way to deal with the "bleeding lead" problem is to start reading the newspaper from the back to the front or to only watch the end of TV news programs. They usually put the good news at the end. And you can always turn the channel—that's one good thing about remote controls!

But before you turn the channel, remember this: The good thing about the bad stuff in the news is that it makes us face all the broken parts of our world. We want you to understand those broken parts and we want you to try and help fix them without becoming broken yourself.

The good thing about the bad stuff in the news is that it makes us face all the broken parts of our world.

In each chapter of this book we will talk about some bad thing you might see or read about in the news. Whenever possible, we'll try to help you understand why that bad thing happens. And we'll try to show you some things you can do—either now or as you grow up—to work with other people to fix that bad thing so that it never happens again. We think that understanding and fixing are the two best ways to get rid of your fears. They're also the two best ways to make the world a better place to live.

Life just isn't perfect yet. Figuring out why that is, and how we can at least make it better, is more than a reason for a book. It's a fine reason for a life.

Good luck and God bless you!

Rabbi Marc Gellman
Monsignor Thomas Hartman

Rethinking
The Security
At Airports

fghan

19 Men Believed to Be Hijac

disturbi

HAT B

No Middle Ground on Terrorism

n Pleads Guilty to R

Millennial Terrorism

ST
BU

INNED RESCUER
THOUSANDS

lls 3 Is

EN

Bombing Suspect Is Said
He Felt 'Duty to Kill Am

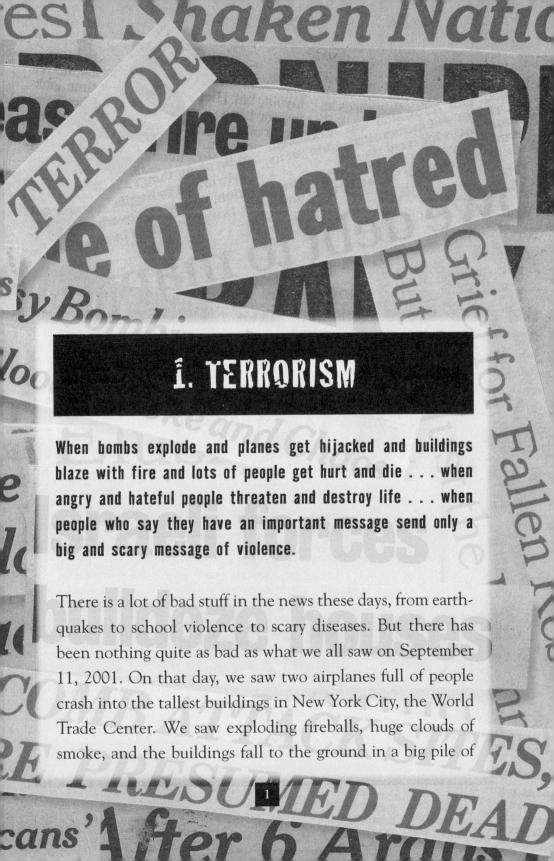

1. TERRORISM

When bombs explode and planes get hijacked and buildings blaze with fire and lots of people get hurt and die . . . when angry and hateful people threaten and destroy life . . . when people who say they have an important message send only a big and scary message of violence.

There is a lot of bad stuff in the news these days, from earthquakes to school violence to scary diseases. But there has been nothing quite as bad as what we all saw on September 11, 2001. On that day, we saw two airplanes full of people crash into the tallest buildings in New York City, the World Trade Center. We saw exploding fireballs, huge clouds of smoke, and the buildings fall to the ground in a big pile of ash and twisted steel. Then we saw the Pentagon building in Washington, D.C., burning because another passenger plane had crashed into it. And we saw a giant smoking pit in the ground near Pittsburgh, where a fourth plane had crashed. More than 3,000 people were killed in just a few minutes on that morning in what are called *terrorist* attacks.

You've probably heard that those four planes were hijacked. That means that some very, very angry people used force to take over the airplanes' controls. You probably asked, like we did, "Why would anyone want to crash a plane? It would kill themselves and hundreds (or thousands) of innocent people!" It's so hard for all of us to understand and answer that question because there's a lot about terrorists and terrorism that we don't understand.

Terrorism happens when people with a certain political cause or religious belief use fear, terror, and violence to try to get other people—usually governments—to do what they want. Sometimes they just threaten to do something bad if they don't get what they want. But they also can kill without a clear reason, and they don't care if there are innocent people in the way. That's because terrorists, the people who use terrorism, are full of big hate.

Terrorism happens when people with a certain political cause or religious belief use fear, terror, and violence to try to get other people to do what they want.

It's hard to explain big hate. Little hate is easy to explain. People hate spinach and hate getting shots and hate when it snows on the weekend instead of on school days. All those hates are little hates. Really they aren't even hates— they're just things you don't like very much. Hate is like a fire that burns up everything good inside you. Some people have a hate that has been burning for so long that they don't care if they kill innocent men, women, and children, and they don't care if they kill themselves. When these haters hook up with other haters, and when they get money and bombs and knives and guns, they can become terrorists.

Terrorism has happened all over the world for many years. You may have heard stories about bombs exploding in places like Ireland, England, Israel, Africa, and other places far, far away. We've been lucky because these awful things haven't happened much in the United States. But terrorism didn't begin in our country on September 11, 2001. In fact, other terrorists attacked the World Trade Center once before, in 1993. That time they killed six people and hurt a thousand with car bombs in one building's garage.

On April 19, 1995, a government building in Oklahoma City was blown up by a terrorist named Timothy McVeigh. His awful act killed 168 people including 19 children, and he did it because he hated the United States government. He did not agree with some of its decisions and thought that his anger gave him the right to blow up innocent people.

In May 1998, Theodore Kaczynski—who some people call the Unabomber—was put in jail for the rest of his life for sending bombs in the mail for over eighteen years to scientists because he feared and hated the things that they were discovering. He thought science was going to hurt our world, but his violence killed three people and badly hurt twenty-nine others.

On August 7, 1998, United States embassies in the African countries of Kenya and Tanzania were blown up by terrorists who hated things that the United States had done that affected their own countries. They killed 257 people and injured 4,074 people. Many of the dead and wounded were African—they were not even citizens of the country that the terrorists hated!

So, as you can see, terrorist attacks have hurt Americans before, and even though they didn't kill as many people as the attack on September 11, they were still horrible events that show us just how deep and awful hate can be.

STUFF TO UNDERSTAND

After terrorist attacks, people get scared and angry. This is normal and natural, and it happens to just about everybody. In fact, it's exactly what the terrorists want. They want us to be scared and they want us to stop living our normal lives. We talked to lots of kids after the September 11 terror attacks who were afraid to fly in an airplane or visit a tall building, or who thought that the terrorists were going to crash a plane into their houses. Maybe you were one of those scared people. We were a little scared, too. In fact, we wrote this so that we could all learn how not to be scared.

You might wonder, if terrorists are angry with a government, why would they hurt all kinds of innocent people who don't run the government? One thing to try to understand is that terrorists usually try to destroy places that have an important meaning to the government and to the country. Most places don't have that special kind of meaning to millions of people, so most places around you are safe and will stay safe. And the few places in the country that *are* very famous and mean a lot to millions of people are being protected more than ever by the police and the government.

When a terrorist strikes, it is such an unusual and horrible thing that you are going to hear tons and tons about it on the news and on the radio wherever you go. And you will probably hear a lot of confusing things. One of the most confusing things you might hear about terrorism is that a lot of times this violence is done by people who say they are acting in the name of religion or in the name of God. If God is good, and if religion is supposed to make people kind and loving, how is this possible?

We think that violence done "in the name of God" is the worst kind of violence because it takes what billions of people all over the world think is good and holy and comforting and creates evil of the worst kind. But sometimes people become so wrapped up in their beliefs and points of view, and they're so sure that they're right, that they truly *believe* God wants it that way. They give themselves the power to do these terrible things by saying that God wants them to do it. But only humans choose to kill other humans in this way, not God.

Also, many terrorists come from places where regular people don't have the same kind of power and freedom that most Americans do. Like gangs that live in cities around us, these terrorists stick together and find ways to create power by scaring and hurting other people. But the ways that they have found are horrible and wrong.

Another thing to remember about terrorism is that, like lots of bad stuff in the news, it's really bad but it's also really *rare*. Terrorist attacks hardly ever happen, even though they are terrible when they do happen. There are lots of bad things in the world that are very rare that don't make you change your life. A few people may have been bitten by sharks, but you will still go into the ocean on a hot summer day. Some people have gotten hit by lightning, but you will still go out in the rain. Some people have gotten hurt or died in car crashes, but you will still get into the car to go to the movies. People sometimes break their legs playing sports, but you will still go skiing.

It's important to be aware of dangers and to try to protect yourself when you can, but you just can't get rid of all the dangers in life. So all of us have a big decision to make: We can hide under our beds all day or we can go on with our lives. It takes courage to go on, but we know that you are brave enough to live your life without always being afraid of the bad stuff in the news.

STUFF YOU CAN FIX

There are a lot of things that need to be fixed in this world in order to get rid of terrorism, but the grown-ups are the ones who need to work on that. In fact, it's the biggest and most important thing our government is working on right now, and there are tens of thousands of people all over the country who are helping them to make our lives safer.

There are three things that you need to get fixed, though: getting rid of your fear, getting through your sadness, and making your insides good and happy instead of letting them get full of anger and hate.

If you still have fear about terrorism, one really good way to let go of some of it is to talk about your fear with your parents and teachers and friends. When you talk about what scares you, you find out that you are not alone. You are like lots of other people who are also scared about what might happen next. Talking about your fears is like letting the air out of a balloon. It lets the fear just whoosh out of you.

When you talk about your fears, you will also find other people who aren't scared, and they will help you understand a whole lot better than we can just why you don't need to worry. Sharing your fears with people you love and trust reminds you that there are people who love you and will protect you. Terrorists only win when we feel scared and alone. By coming together with our friends and family, with members of our church or synagogue or mosque, or just with our neighbors, we remember that we are part of something bigger than us that will not let us down.

There is an old saying that "Sticks alone can be broken by a child. Sticks in a bundle are unbreakable." You can try this out for yourself. Take one pencil and try to break it. It's easy, isn't it? Now take five or six pencils and try to break them. You can't do it because the bunch of pencils is so much stronger than just one pencil alone. When people are alone they also are weak and can break easily. But when we are together in communities or families or groups of friends, we are unbreakable. We become a million times stronger than when each of us is alone.

Even if you're not afraid, watching all of this bad stuff on TV might make you feel sad. You probably see that your parents are sad. Just seeing all of the sad people you don't know on TV might make you feel sad! We think it's okay to feel sad, because sadness is the price of love. When we love and care for others—even people we don't know—it hurts when they die. It even hurts when they are just feeling down. But it's better to love people and feel sad sometimes than not to love people at all. If we don't love others, we will become full of hate—like criminals and terrorists.

If you or someone you know has had a terrible loss in this violence, it's important that you talk to grown-ups around you about your sadness. It's the same as talking to them about your fears—it lets the sadness whoosh right out of you like air from a balloon. There are many special people who will want to help you do this—rabbis, ministers, priests, teachers, counselors, or doctors. It may take a while to get over the hurt, and so you'll need to be patient with yourself. And if your sadness doesn't last as long as the sadness of your family or friends, that's okay, too. We think it's very important that you go on with the very big and great job of having fun and being a kid while the grown-ups work on fixing the bad stuff in the news.

There's one more thing you can do as a kid to help good people win over the terrorists. You can try to keep hate out of you. Since most people believed that it was some Muslim guys from the Middle East who crashed those jets into the World Trade Center and the Pentagon, after the attack some people started to talk about how much they hated Arabs. We even heard about kids beating up Arab, Pakistani, and Palestinian kids, and kids who are Muslim. This reaction is mean, unfair, and wrong—it's *very* wrong.

Timothy McVeigh was a white guy from New York state who called himself a Christian, and after he bombed a government building, nobody said, "I hate white guys from New York" or "I hate Christians." It doesn't make sense to hate a whole group for what just a few people have done. Also, remember that some people that you may think are part of a certain group may not even call themselves a part of that group. It's not your job or our job to judge others—

that's the job of God (and those people who wear long robes and work in courthouses)!

Hate is like poison to your insides. Hating somebody else is like drinking poison and expecting another person to die. Hate hurts you and kills the best that's in you, and that's why you should try to keep hate out of your heart. It may be okay to fight against evil, but it's not okay to become hateful and evil when fighting for what's right. Keeping yourself good inside is the first big step to making the world good outside.

Believe it or not, there *is* something that everyone agrees is good about these awful terrorist attacks. Seeing the worst in bad people brings out the best in good people. After September 11, people came from all over America to help out in New York City and Washington, D.C. Some came to dig and some came to heal, some came to make food and some came to give out clean clothes. These people worked for free and they worked day and night, all because the bad thing had brought out the good in them. Nobody ever wants to see bad things happen, but when they do, it's very important not to just see the blood and hear the crying. It's also important to see the helpers and listen to the singing and cheering.

There are lots of great things about living now. You can e-mail friends all over the world. You can get on an airplane and go just about anywhere and get there fast. You can live in big cities with lots of things to do and places to go and jobs to do. You can watch TV and see what's happening everywhere, and you can even check your math homework on a calculator! Living in the world today has a lot of good things in it for sure.

But living in our modern times has bad stuff in it, too. Terrorists are one of the worst bad things in our world, but as bad as they are, they cannot change the good things. They cannot change the good people and they cannot win. On days like September 11, 2001, it's hard to believe that the good people will win. But the best news is that God made the world so that there are many, many more good people than bad people. Right now and in all the days to come, good people are getting organized and will find the bad people and protect you from them.

Remember Adolf Hitler? Hitler took over Austria and Poland and Holland and Belgium and Norway and Czechoslovakia and France and Yugoslavia AND Greece before America even got into the war, but he still lost big. Bad people usually get a head start on good people, but they never win the race.

You see, the world is made in such a way that when you drop something, it always falls down. That's called the law of gravity. But the world is also made so that life always wins over death, hope always wins over sadness, and the good people always win over the bad people. The good doesn't always win right away and it doesn't always win without a fight, but it always wins!

8th-grad

Police Say Student Gunman
Was Seeking School Official

4, Arrested Aft

ers in Talking of Teenager

Legal Action
After Killing
At Schools
Often Fails

Threats of Scho

Explosion Kills 41 in S

School

hooting

Student Held in Shootings

2. KIDS KILLING KIDS

When kids bring guns to school and shoot people for no reason . . . when kids beat other kids . . . when school doesn't seem safe anymore.

Maybe you remember seeing stories on the news about kids who just came to school one day with guns and shot people. Sometimes they hunted down certain teachers or students they hated, and sometimes they just shot whoever got in their way. Some of the teachers and students who were shot died. Some lived but were badly hurt. But everyone in these schools was terrified, and everyone who saw the stories on the news was really scared.

The stories caused everyone to ask the same question:

"Why would kids kill kids?" People aren't as shocked when criminals and drug dealers and gang members kill people because they want to rob them or hurt them or get them to join their gangs, but nobody expects children who have never hurt anybody to suddenly go on a shooting spree.

What is even more confusing and frightening is that the kids who did the killings often seemed like normal, regular kids. They usually came from normal families and they went to normal schools, and they had usually never hurt anyone before the day they brought the guns to school. These kids were among the least likely murderers in America. So what went wrong? Teachers, parents, and students were left wondering if they had missed some sign that the kids were about to become killers. People blamed themselves or others for not taking seriously these kids' "jokes" or threats before the shootings.

After the shootings, lots of kids were afraid to go to school. They saw that the people who did the shootings looked like kids they knew, and the schools looked like their schools. And it wasn't just kids who were afraid. Many parents were afraid to send their children to school. Teachers and principals were worried about how they could make their schools safer, and how they could spot signs that a kid was about to become a killer. Even though fewer than thirty kids were killed in school in the United States between 1999 and 2001, the fear about the killings reached almost every home and every school in America.

Even the TV newspeople who reported the school shootings started to ask themselves questions about how they report the news. After some of the shootings, kids in others schools imitated those crimes by shooting (or by planning to hurt) people in their own schools. These are called copycat crimes. Many people wondered if the news stories actually caused more shootings by giving kids ideas they didn't have before. The media didn't know how to respond. On the one hand, these were important stories that had to be reported, but on the other hand, had reporting them so heavily caused even more problems?

STUFF TO UNDERSTAND

The first thing to understand is that going to school is *still* the safest and smartest thing you can do as a kid. The fact that some cars crash doesn't mean that you won't ride in a car again. The fact that some planes crash doesn't mean that you'll never fly in a plane again. And even though in SOME schools SOME kids shot SOME other kids, it doesn't mean that you have to be afraid to go to school again. Millions of kids go to school every day and go home at night and put on their pajamas and brush their teeth and say their prayers and NOTHING bad happens to them . . . aside from maybe forgetting to do their math homework and getting in trouble for it the next day.

Of course, nothing is *totally* safe. People slip in their own bathtubs and people trip over their own feet. Part of life is accepting good risks and avoiding bad risks. Going to school is a good risk. It's also a low risk, and it's one that's very important for your future. Jumping off a bridge with a rubber band tied to your ankles while you scream on your way down to a river with big jagged rocks and then having the rubber band pull you back up into the air at just the last second before you splatter your guts all over the rocks is a BAD risk!

> **Part of life is accepting good risks and avoiding bad risks.**

Just because everything we do in life has some risk tied to it doesn't mean that all risks are the same. "Odds" means "the chance that something will happen." If your parents buy a lottery ticket, the odds of their winning the big jackpot are about "fifty million to one." This means that probably only one time out of fifty million tries would they actually *win* the lottery. These are "long odds." On the other hand, if you flip a coin, the odds of it coming up heads are "two to one," which means that about half the time you flip the coin it will probably come up heads and about half the time it will probably come up tails. These are "short odds." The odds of something bad happening to you in school are really, really long—longer than winning the lottery. Life doesn't give you a promise that the really bad stuff will *never* happen to you, but you do have short odds that everything will be all right. That should be enough to ease your mind and let you get on with the great and exciting job of being a kid.

Even though the odds of a school shooting are long, after the shootings, many schools did things to make safe schools even safer. Some schools put in metal detectors so that a kid who might try to bring a gun or a knife to school would be caught. School counselors and teachers are on the lookout for kids who seem lonely, depressed, or angry, and any threat that they hear from any student in their school is taken very seriously. These days, kids who say something threatening as a joke might suddenly find themselves in the back of a police car headed to jail. Many of the signs that people missed about the kids who did the shootings in the past are not being missed today.

Even though schools are getting safer, it's still important to try to understand the reasons for the killings: Those kids who did the killing had a huge bucket of pain inside of them. You know what outside pain is: When you cut your finger, break your arm, fall out of a tree, or drop something heavy on your foot, you feel outside pain. That outside pain might be really bad, but it goes away when the hurt part of you heals. But there's also *inside* pain that many people feel every day, and it takes this kind of pain a much longer time to go away. Inside pain comes from feeling scared and lonely, from feeling that nobody loves you or cares about what happens to you.

Feeling unloved or lonely is the worst feeling a human being can have. It's like putting a plant that needs light in a dark closet. It's like taking a fish out of water. Loneliness is like an acid that eats right through your soul. The kids who shot other kids were lonely and broken by their inside pain. They were not the "cool kids." They had very few friends— if any at all. They felt that nobody cared about them. They felt like invisible people, and they were angry. That's why they did what they did. Some of them figured that if they brought guns to school and shot people, everybody would notice them. How could anyone ignore them? They thought that if they killed the people in their school who didn't like them, their pain would go away. But violence is a sick and broken and cruel way of trying to be noticed and trying to be loved.

> **Feeling unloved or lonely is the worst feeling a human being can have.**

Inside pain, like outside pain, is a normal part of being alive. The problem is that some people just don't have anybody to help them or heal them or share their pain.

Being in pain is no fun, but it's also usually no big deal. Being in pain when you feel totally alone is a huge deal. Being sad all of the time is probably the worst pain a person can feel.

When somebody has outside pain from a broken arm, it's easy to see that they're hurting. They have a big cast on their arm, a sign that they're broken and need to heal up. But when a person isn't loved enough and feels totally alone, it's sometimes hard to see that kind of pain. And when someone has so much inside pain that they can't take it anymore, they can just snap.

Not everybody who has inside pain ends up hurting people. The inside pain some kids feel can also cause them to hurt themselves and not others. Every year over 4,000 young people commit suicide. Kids hurt themselves for the very same reasons that they hurt others—it's all a way to try to get rid of their huge bucket of inside pain. Unless those broken and suffering kids can find a way to heal, they're a danger to themselves and a danger to those around them.

The causes of inside pain are different for each person, but there are some big things that cause a lot of hurt. One is feeling different. Maybe you feel fat, or maybe you're not good in sports, or maybe you don't have the money to buy the stuff that the popular kids buy. Maybe you're really shy or maybe you're really into your studies or maybe you look a little goofy to some people. Maybe you're not really different at all, but you just feel different for some deep and personal reason. Feeling different can cut you off from other people—and when you're cut off, you can lose touch with the whole world.

Sometimes kids don't feel love because their families are broken. A difficult divorce or the death of a parent can sometimes break a family apart. But these aren't the only broken families. The much bigger reason for broken families is parents who have no time for their kids. When parents work too long, travel too much, drink too much, or go out with their friends too much, kids are not only left alone, they're left out. Being left out of your parents' lives or their love is a terrible thing that can cause a lot of inside pain.

Kids can be from broken families even if they have a healthy mom and dad and a big house with a little white dog. Some of the killers were from homes where there was enough money but not enough love. Giving toys and pres-

Kids can be from broken families even if they have a healthy mom and dad and a big house with a little white dog.

ents and stuff is no replacement for love. When we say "love," we don't just mean hugging and kissing. And love doesn't just mean giving a kid food, clothes, a bike, and a computer. Parents show love for their children when they set limits and say no sometimes and teach the difference between right and wrong. Kids who are loved are not perfect. They can make bad choices and do bad things. The difference between loved kids and lonely kids is that the loved kids are much more likely to learn from their bad choices and learn how to choose better next time.

Now, just because a person feels lonely doesn't mean that he or she will hurt other people. Understanding why kids have killed other kids doesn't mean that what they did was okay. What they did was cruel and wrong. They destroyed lives that were just getting going. They took children away from their parents and from the whole world—forever. They need to be punished for what they did, and their parents need to figure out how they raised a kid who had no idea that life is definitely not theirs to take.

STUFF YOU CAN FIX

You may not think that you can do anything to stop a kid from killing other kids, but you may not be right. There are some things you can do that just might help out a kid who is in real trouble. One easy thing you could do is to ask a kid who is eating lunch alone to eat lunch with you and your friends. It may seem small, but asking a shy or lonely kid to join you for lunch might be just the thing to convince that person that somebody cares about him or her. If that kid feels less lonely, maybe he will feel less angry, and if he feels less angry, maybe he will feel less inside pain. A simple act of kindness can go a long way.

A simple act of kindness can go a long way.

Another thing you can do about school violence is to never let the bad stuff you hear go unreported. If you hear some kid threatening to hurt teachers or other students, or threatening to bring a gun to school, you need to let some adult know about it. We know that ratting on a friend is a hard thing to do, and no kid wants to get a reputation as a snitch. But if something bad happens and you heard about it ahead of time, you'll not only feel terrible, you could also be in trouble with the police or your school. What you need now is a plan about what you'll do if you hear that something bad might happen at school.

One plan you might choose is to tell your parents. This is a good plan because it gives you a chance to talk things over with the people you love and trust the most and who love and trust you the most. If they think the stuff you heard is bad enough, they can talk to the principal of your school. Nobody would ever know that it was you who reported it.

Another plan is to tell a teacher you trust. Principals might believe teachers they know well more than parents they don't know well. Maybe the best person to tell is the school psychologist or guidance counselor, since it's their job to make sure that the students in the school are okay. The main thing you need to know is that there are people in your life or in your school who can help you so that you don't have to deal with hearing scary stuff alone.

Some kids can't deal with the idea of getting their friends in trouble and refuse to tell anybody anything. If you're like that, one thing you might do is confront the person making the threats. If they say that they're "just kidding"—as most of the killers said to kids who confronted them—you can say something like this: "Well, I hope you're kidding, but let me tell you something. I don't think it's funny. You're freaking me out. If I hear it again, I'm gonna tell somebody!" This plan takes courage, but it takes you off the hook for being a snitch because you warned the kid first. If it was just a sick joke, the kid will probably stop, but if the talk continues, you can and should do something about it the next time you hear it.

One of the only good things to come out of the school shootings is that nowadays most kids would never blame another kid for telling on a student who made threats at school. Kids who have made threats have been kicked out of school, and have gotten the message that joking about hurting kids or teachers can get you into big trouble. So don't worry about telling. The biggest danger you face is in *not* telling.

Fixing kids shooting other kids also means fixing the problem of guns. Some kids who killed got their guns from unlocked gun cabinets in their homes. Some used older friends to buy them at gun shows where the gun sellers don't check on the gun buyers very carefully. What to do about guns is one of those things that causes a lot of arguing in America.

The biggest danger you face is in NOT telling a grown-up about threats or jokes that make you nervous.

Everybody agrees that kids should never bring guns to school, but people do not agree on how to prevent it. Some people think that we should make guns illegal for everybody or make guns really hard to buy. Other people say that there are enough laws against guns right now, and we just need to help the police enforce the laws we already have. Some people think that every gun should have a trigger lock so that even if a kid steals it from home, the gun can't be fired without the key to the lock. It's not our job to tell you who is right. It's your job to learn about the problem of gun control, and as you get older, decide for yourself what is the right thing to do.

Another thing you might want to think about is the way you deal with your own anger. You've probably lost your temper before, or maybe you have done something hurtful or cruel to somebody else. Think about why you did it. What was the inside pain that made you so angry that you lashed out at someone else? Is that pain still there? If the answer is yes, maybe you should talk to somebody about it.

We all have some kind of inside pain. Most of us can deal with it, but for kids who kill, that pain is so big it breaks them down. If we can try to understand their pain, we might better understand the other kinds of pain that break kids and that break our world.

Lawyers

State and F

Stalls a Heal

OUR T
POOR,

Homeless in America: they're sick, they're
and they're under 12. Can we live with that

Red
the
Lives Held
ing
Uninsured

ED, OUR
UR KIDS

Sea

3. HUNGER NEAR AND FAR

When you see starving children who look like skeletons with big eyes . . . when you see people sleeping in refrigerator boxes . . . when kids have no money for lunch . . . when poverty stares you right in the face.

Maybe there aren't enough video games for every kid in the world, and maybe there aren't enough scooters or stereos, baseball mitts, tennis rackets, or designer jeans for every kid in the world, and all of this is no big deal. But there should be enough food in the world for every hungry kid and for every hungry person, and if there isn't . . . *it's a very big deal!* It's a shame and it's a disgrace— some people would say it's a sin—for so many people in a world with so much food to be so very, very hungry.

You probably don't really see starvation in your life. You wake up and eat breakfast and go to school and come home and do your homework or go to a friend's to play and then you go to sleep and get ready for another day. But if you watch the bad stuff on the news, you'll see it a lot. The news might be covering a war or a famine or some other horrible thing and then you'll see starving people staring right at you from your TV. Sometimes starving people look like walking skeletons. They have sunken eyes and bones that you can see poking out under their skin. They can be kind of scary-looking, but they also look sad. They seem to stare at you with big sad eyes and say: "I am starving and I am going to die. You have more food in your refrigerator now than I eat in a year. Can you help me, please?"

If you wonder just how many people are starving in this world, here are some numbers. We got them from our friend Bill Ayres, who runs World Hunger Year. He knows more about the problem of hunger than anyone we know.

In the world:

- There are about six billion people here on planet earth, and every night about 800 million of them go to bed hungry.
- Every single day 40,000 people on planet earth die of starvation or diseases that come from being

hungry. That means 1,666 people die every hour of every day of every year because they do not have enough food to eat and they get sick and die.

- In the last fifty years almost 400 million people have died of hunger. That's three times more than all the people killed in all the wars during the last 100 years.

In America:

- Over 32.2 million people (12.1 million of them are children) live below the poverty line. That means a family of four must live on *less than $17,029 a year!* That comes to a little less than twelve dollars a day to pay for everything in your life—food, clothing, housing, health care, transportation, electric bills—everything! Some kids get that much each day just to pay for lunch, ice cream, soda, and video games.
- Two million people a year are homeless.

On Long Island where we live, which is right near New York City:

- Each night 300,000 people go to bed hungry.
- There are over 400 soup kitchens and food pantries on Long Island where people come who don't have any money to buy food.

- The groups that fight hunger near where we live on Long Island collect over three million pounds of food per year from restaurants, country clubs, and party places, and that three million pounds of food isn't even enough to feed all the hungry people here on Long Island.

You might be surprised if you found out the number of hungry people near where you live.

STUFF TO UNDERSTAND

Being hungry usually happens because you're poor, but it's not the only thing that can happen to you when you're poor. You can get sick because the little food you do get isn't healthy food. You can also get sick because you have no money to see a doctor, or you can get sick because you're not always clean, or you get sick because you don't get enough sleep in a safe place that you can call your home. You also might not get a good education because you probably live in a place with bad schools or you don't even live in one place long enough to go to school. This means you can't go to college or even get a good job, so if your family is poor, the chances of you being poor when you grow up are very great. And then there's the problem of getting hurt, or even killed. Poor people sometimes live in places where they have no protection from gangs and drug addicts and criminals. So you see, being hungry is only one of many bad things that can happen to you when you're poor.

Even though it's so hard to see starving children on the news, in a way it's a good thing that we do. If we didn't see starving people on TV, we wouldn't see them at all. We wouldn't have to try to understand why they're poor and what we can do to help them. They force us to see the broken parts of our world, and hopefully they make us so angry that we may try to get together with our friends and family and religious groups and do something about what we just saw. The news wakes us up, even if we want to sleep through it and turn our backs on the world's problems. The news will not let us turn away.

One of the reasons many people don't do much to try to fix bad stuff is that we live our lives so that we don't have to see the bad stuff. We build roads that go around the parts of our cities where poor people live so we don't have to see them. We like to live in cities or suburbs or towns where most of the people who live near us are like us. And if you live in a big city, you might see homeless people sleeping in old boxes or on benches, but you can just walk right by them or even step over them on the sidewalk. You don't know them, and you may not ever see them again!

We live apart from poor people, even when we live near them. This separation from the poor leads people to think bad things about the poor. You probably hear that poor people are lazy and that they should just get jobs. Or you hear that they're drug addicts or alcoholics and spend all their money on drugs or booze. Or you hear that they're crazy. But you probably have no idea what is true or false because you don't know them.

We live apart from poor people, even when we live near them.

First of all, one thing you should know is that lots of people who come to soup kitchens are already working. They're just working at jobs that don't pay them enough money. To live and raise your family, you need to make enough money to pay rent, get to work, buy some clothes to wear, pay for electricity and heat, pay for a phone, get medical insurance for your family, and buy food. If you have a family of four people, you need to make between $25,000 and $35,000 a year to survive without help. If you're making the minimum wage, you're just making about $226 a week—which is only $11,700 a year. This means that even if both parents work all day every week, even *together* they don't make enough to pay for all the things their family needs to get by. And this doesn't even include paying taxes or paying for child care. If you live in a place where things are expensive, you're really in trouble.

At the time we wrote this book, the government had said that $17,029 a year or less is the poverty level for a family of four. But $17,029 is nowhere *near* enough money to support a family of four. So, many working people have to choose between buying food or paying the rent. That's why people come to soup kitchens where they can get good, free food for their families.

Some people may not make enough money even to pay the rent. But if you have no home because you have no money, you can't wash up and put on clean clothes for a job interview, and you can't get money from the government if you don't have an address to send it to. Once you're home-less, it's very hard to get off the street. In most cities, there are places called shelters where people can go and sleep so that they don't have to stay on the street and sleep in old refrigerator boxes. But while all of the shelters for homeless people are warm, some of them are not nice. Some can be dangerous places where people may be attacked or robbed during the night. It's sad when someone must choose between a shelter and the street.

It's true that there are some people living on the street who have mental problems. But they don't have money to pay for help from a psychiatrist or psychologist. Many cities don't have enough mental hospitals or social workers to care for everyone who needs help, and so these broken people are left to wander the streets. Some of them hurt other people, some of them hurt themselves, and some of them die in the streets.

Now, we're not saying that every poor person is a victim. Some may be bums and a few may actually be criminals, but most of the people on the street or eating in the soup kitchens are just like you and me except that they really need a helping hand. Many children who are poor and hungry just want a place to be warm and safe, a place to learn, and a chance to grow up. After you see how many poor people *want* to get better but can't, it makes you angry. It makes you want to try to fix some part of this big problem.

STUFF YOU CAN FIX

We know that you can't make poverty go away. Even if you were a grown-up, you alone couldn't make it go away.

Poverty happens for many different reasons. Sometimes countries have too many people and not enough food, or enough food but too many wars, or they have people in power who steal all of the good stuff for themselves. Or sometimes, like in America, when people can't find jobs, they just get left behind. As you grow up, you can learn about the different causes of poverty and explore the ways to fix these problems with other people who feel the same way.

The one thing you can do now, even as a kid, is to give some of your time and effort to help the hunger organizations working in your town. There's no place so rich that there are *no* hungry people nearby, and you can start out by helping them in your spare time. You can volunteer at a soup kitchen or a food pantry where people come to get healthful, free food for themselves and their families.

Or maybe you can get kids and teachers at your school to help organize a hunger program. You could collect food, you could write about hunger in your school paper, or you could make posters about hunger. You could even invite someone from a hunger organization to come to your school and talk about the problems of hunger and homelessness. You could wash cars or sell pancakes or collect pennies in a big jug and use the money to help a local soup kitchen. It's amazing how fast those pennies add up. In a school near us, kids raised over $40,000 for hunger causes just by throwing their pennies into one big barrel!

We also know kids who have had big parties where they've asked their guests to bring food or presents to give to hunger organizations instead of gifts for themselves. You would be surprised at how many great ideas you can come up with on your own.

One of the best places to do things to help hungry people is at your church or synagogue or mosque. In the places we pray to God, we remember that everything we have is just loaned to us by God, and we're supposed to share the extra stuff with people who have not been given enough.

Working with the poor helps them now and it changes you forever. After you work in a soup kitchen giving hungry people the only good meal they will have all day, you don't complain as much about all the stuff you don't have. After

Working with the poor helps them now and it changes you forever.

you see kids who have to sleep in a car, you won't complain about sharing your room. After you see kids with no mom or dad, you'll thank God for yours even when they tell you to take out the garbage. None of us really understands how good we have it until we see people who pretty much have nothing.

> **None of us really understands how good we have it until we see people who pretty much have nothing.**

We help a group called Island Harvest, which collects leftover food from restaurants, supermarkets, country clubs, and places where people go to have big parties. This food would normally be thrown into the garbage because it can't be served again at locations where people pay for food, but volunteers pick it up and bring it to the soup kitchens where it's really needed. Working at Island Harvest, we've seen things that made our hearts break. One day one of the volunteers asked a little girl with dirty hair and sad sunken eyes if she had eaten breakfast. She said, "It wasn't my turn to eat today." A family should never have to take turns to eat!

We also remember a little girl named Maria who came to the soup kitchen on a day when one of our Island Harvest drivers had picked up some bread and a birthday cake from Walter's Black Forest Bake Shop. The birthday cake had been ordered but never picked up. That day little

Maria walked into the soup kitchen and walked right past the meat loaf and the mashed potatoes, past the salad and the bread, past the juice and the cookies, and just stood there, her eyes wide open, staring at the birthday cake. She looked up at the driver, who had just put the cake on the table, and said, "How did you know today was my birthday?" Maria had never had a birthday cake, but she had one that day.

You may think that doing any of this just doesn't matter because the problem of hunger is so big on this planet and you're so small on this planet. Well, we read a story in a book by Loren Eiseley that gives us hope when we feel that way:

A young man was jogging on the beach one morning when he saw an old man ahead of him bending down and picking up starfish and throwing them into the sea one by one. As he came close, the young man asked, "What are you doing?" The old man answered, "There was a storm last night and many starfish were washed high up onto the beach. If I don't throw them back, the sun will kill them by noon." The young man laughed and said, "You're a fool, old man. The beach is miles long and there are thousands of starfish stranded on it. You can't get to them all before the sun drys them out. What you're doing just doesn't matter." The old man threw another starfish into the safety of the waves and said, "It mattered to that one!"

Iowa Town Does Bat

Effects Linger

of Relief and Gasps at E

Cost in Western Was

No More She

Stealthy Tornado

Storm Bri

m.p.h. are expe

Mississippi Ri

Continues to R

Two Days After

4. THE WILD EARTH

When you see pictures of a house floating down the street . . . when you see towns crumbled up in an earthquake . . . when forest fires burn trees and animals and houses for miles and miles . . . when the earth looks wild, mean, and very scary.

The bad stuff in the news isn't always news of people being hurt by other people. Sometimes the news is about people being hurt by Mother Nature. While we were writing this book, a big earthquake hit northern India and killed almost 20,000 people. That night we saw pictures on television of people crying and buildings crushed like they were made of sand. Those pictures were full of dirt and death. And they're especially scary because there's nothing anybody can do to stop a tragedy like this one from happening.

You might not be living in a place where earthquakes usually happen, but you're probably living in a place where *something* could happen. Maybe you live near a river that could flood and carry your house down the street and into the next town. Maybe you live near a volcano that could erupt and send melted rocks down on your backyard and cook your tomatoes even before you pick them. Maybe you live where tornadoes that can pick up cars and cows and old ladies riding on bicycles blow across the land, or where mud slides destroy trees and houses and people, or where avalanches of snow bury anybody and anything in their way. People get hit by lightning and drowned by storms and starved by droughts. Nature brings us food and water and wood and air, but sometimes Nature takes away everything it has given in an instant.

What blows everyone away about the bad stuff from Nature is that it's usually really hard to tell when it will happen, and nobody can stop it from happening. Modern technology is very good, but it isn't good enough to tell us *exactly* where, or when, or how big the next earthquake will be. This is hard for some people to accept. They say, "Hey, we sent men to the moon, why can't we figure out the earth?" You would think that with all of our science, supercomputers, and all of our smart people, we could do better at warning people to get out of the way of some big boom, squish, snap, or blow that Mother Nature has decided to send our way.

A lot of times it's God who gets the bad rap for Mother Nature's madness. People can understand the bad stuff that comes from bad people doing bad things, but so much suffering comes from Nature. If God made Nature and God is supposedly so good, then what gives here? How can a good God send such bad things to people who are not doing much of anything wrong?

STUFF TO UNDERSTAND

Sometimes it's hard to watch the way Nature works because Nature can look so cruel: the way lions kill antelopes, the way insects can destroy a whole forest of trees, the way fire can rip across the land, and the way so many living things die every minute of every day is sad and scary to see.

It's okay to be afraid of the stuff you see in Nature. We know what that's like: We've hidden under the covers during lightning storms, and we've been scared when big winds almost blew us off our feet. We puked our guts out when we were caught on a boat in bad weather. And sometimes when the lights went out and the wind was making ghostly noises in the trees, we have been afraid.

Some of these fears left us as we grew up, but others stay with us. We once saw a woman hanging on to a rope in a flood, and we knew there was no way she could fight the power of water. We have seen people dug out from under collapsed houses and we have had our own nightmares about being buried under mud, being burned under lava and ash from a volcano, or drowning at sea. All these fears are normal and natural. They come from understanding that Nature is far more powerful than any of us. Facing your fear is a good thing because it can make you more careful. It can also lead you to help other frightened people face life here on planet earth with hope and courage.

The plan of Nature is in perfect balance. In Nature there's as much life as death, as much springtime as winter, as much beauty and happiness as hurting and devastation. Everything that's burned or squished or blown away or that dies of old age just rots, goes back into the earth, and gives the earth food for new life. Even though earthquakes and volcanoes can bring death, they're also a sign of a living earth that moves, cracks, and breathes. Hurricanes, floods, and lightning storms also come from the way the earth breathes.

Weather, even bad weather, is also a sign that the earth is alive. Our weather makes cold and hot air move around the world, and when the cold and hot air crash together, storms happen. It's very sad when these storms hurt people, but there's nothing bad about a storm. They bring new rain and new life to parts of the earth that are dry. Forest fires are a scary thing that can happen when the earth is too dry. But forest fires also create open spaces where new life can grow with the help of nutrients that come from burned trees. The smoke from these fires can clear forests of bad insects and disease. Some pine trees have seeds that only open in a fire! If you only think about how much death there is in Nature, you miss half the picture. The other half of the picture is life.

> **If you only think about how much death there is in Nature, you miss half the picture. The other half of the picture is life.**

Remembering that Nature gives as much life as it takes also helps us let go of anger toward God. We believe that God gives life and God takes life away. If you just believe in Nature and not God, that's fine with us. Whatever you believe, you'll come to understand someday that the world is full of life and death, and that our job is to be thankful for all the life we get and to be ready for death when it comes. Nature was not created to give you only sunny days and calm seas, only peaceful rivers and fruit-filled fields. Nature is life, so being angry at Nature is like being angry at life. It's a waste of time.

Even though science can't stop or change Nature, it's a very good thing for science to keep trying to understand how Nature works. Scientists keep trying to predict the weather better and farther in advance. Scientists are working on instruments that can be buried near earthquake centers to help figure out what the earth is doing and when it's doing it. Satellites can track hurricanes now and can help give earlier warnings to ships and people who live near the coastlines. Avalanche scientists know how to create small avalanches to prevent huge avalanches. Flood-control scientists are always inventing new ways to send flood waters away from cities. Irrigation scientists are figuring out ways to get water to dry areas and to recycle the water we have already used.

All of these scientists are using their tools and brains to figure out how we can protect ourselves from the bad stuff that comes from Nature. When you think about what you might want to do with your life, think about being a scientist and working on ways to understand Nature and keep people safe!

STUFF YOU CAN FIX

There's definitely nothing we can do to fix the earth's natural cycles! But knowing that is a good thing. It helps us to stay humble. We have been able to conquer Nature in so many ways that sometimes we think we can control anything and do anything. Night doesn't stop us because we have electric lights. Cold doesn't stop us because we have heaters. Heat doesn't stop us because we have air conditioners. But Nature is still stronger than us. Remembering this helps us to respect the earth and Nature, and it helps us to be modest about what we have learned and what we have built.

Believe it or not, there's another good thing that comes from our struggles with natural disasters. When Nature slams us, people pull together and help one another.

After the earthquake in India, people sent food, clothes, and medicine, and doctors went there to help the sick and injured. Governments sent money, tents, planes, and machines to help dig out the ruined cities. And the same thing happens after hurricanes, tornadoes, or floods. The Red Cross, Doctors Without Borders, and other relief organizations show us that people have a big and deep need to help other people. Sometimes, when life is too comfortable, people can be very selfish and care only about their own family and friends, but when things are really bad, the really good parts of human beings come out.

You can help if a disaster strikes. You can organize food or clothing pickups in your school, or help raise money for the organizations doing the relief work. You can pray for the people who have lost their homes and their loved ones. And you can talk to your family about sending stuff to help. After Hurricane Andrew hit Florida in 1992, many churches and synagogues and families and just plain ordinary folks drove down there to help clean up and fix up and care for the people who had been left homeless or hurt. But the stuff they brought to the victims of the hurricane was not as important as the message they brought. This was the message: "Don't worry, you're not alone."

Too bad it takes a disaster to bring out the best in us, but it's still great to see how the good in us can win. Sometimes all it takes is a big storm.

Derailment **atality**

Kills Passenger and Injures 96

Toddler Is Killed by a School Bus in Brooklyn

Cra

blast spurs bus

Five Are

Two military jets

third crashes in

Plane Crash in a Backyard

5. CRASH, SMASH & BURN

When you see pieces of an airplane floating in the water or scattered in a field . . . when a ship sinks and people drown . . . when a train goes off the tracks . . . when cars crash and kill people . . . when the things we build to help us end up hurting us.

Some of the scariest bad stuff in the news are crash stories. Sometimes it's a plane that crashes. Sometimes a train or a bus or a car or a motorcycle or a truck or a boat or a helicopter or a ski lift or an elevator or a bike or a roller coaster or . . . well, you get the idea. Anything we ride on or ride in can crash and hurt us or kill us. The bigger and faster the thing, the more chance there is that if it crashes, people will be killed. And when some big traveling machine crashes and kills people, you're going to see it on the news.

When crash stories show up on the news, it's natural to be sad and scared. We feel sad for the hurt people and for the families of the people who died. And we're scared because we know that someday we'll probably ride in the same thing that just crashed and burned, and then we start thinking a lot about how awful it would be to fall from the sky in a burning plane or sink in a boat or crash in a car.

Crash stories on the news can make us think that maybe we should never fly in a plane again or ride in a car again or travel somewhere on a train or on a boat ever again. These are natural feelings, but they're terrible feelings of fear. No way to die is good, but dying in a crash seems like one of the worst ways to go.

> Crash stories on the news can make us think that maybe we should never fly in a plane again or ride in a car again or travel somewhere on a train or a boat again.

We're both clergy guys. We often bury people who have died. We're used to seeing death—at least that's what we thought. Then one day back in 1996 we got a call from the governor of New York, who told us that TWA Flight 800 had just crashed into the Atlantic Ocean, killing all 230 people on board. When we arrived on the scene, there were pieces of the plane still burning in the water. Some ordinary people did some very extraordinary things on that terrible night of the crash. They drove their boats as fast as they could out to the crash site. Some people found bodies or pieces of bodies floating in the water and brought them into their boats, covered them with blankets, and brought them ashore. They cried, horrified at what they saw, but they went out again and again to look for anybody who might have survived.

There was a big funeral service for all the families of the people who died in the crash. We were there and helped lead the service of prayer. Looking out at hundreds of sobbing families trying to deal with this tragedy was almost more than we could bear. We met a grandma who was holding a little baby. The baby's mother and father and older sister and brother had all been killed in the crash. That grandma knew she had to raise that baby now, and she didn't know if she had the strength. She was going to try, but she was broken in a deep place. When you see so much death in such a small place, it takes your breath away.

And all this death happened because we have invented big machines to help lots of people travel to far places all over the world. And when one of those machines crashes, hundreds of people are killed in just seconds. On most days it seems like a good thing to have these machines. But it did not seem like a good thing on the beach that day looking into the eyes of hundreds of people whose lives would never be the same.

STUFF TO UNDERSTAND

The first thing to understand about crashes is that you can usually trust the things you ride or fly or float in. Even though they all can break and crash, it doesn't happen that often. (Remember long odds and short odds from Chapter Two? We're talking about long odds here.)

Plane crashes make the biggest news because they kill the most people. But it's an amazing thing to think of how many flights don't crash, and how many people get from here to there every day with no problems at all (except maybe when the airlines lose your luggage). Millions of people fly in thousands of airplanes and get to a zillion places safely. Nothing is totally safe, but flying is pretty darned safe. Even when planes crash, it's possible for some people to survive the crash. We were told by airline safety people that most people in airplane accidents actually do survive. Not all crashes are like TWA Flight 800, where everybody died.

Millions of people fly in thousands of airplanes and get to a zillion places safely.

Cars crash more than planes, but even cars don't crash that much when you think about how many trips people take. And because of seat belts, air bags, and car seats, the number of people who are hurt and killed in car crashes is going down every year. The same thing is true of train crashes and boat accidents. The machines we build to take us from here to there are mostly very safe.

Just remember the odds. Odds are the chances that something will happen. And the odds that you'll crash in a plane or car or train are very long odds. What this means is that the chances of something bad happening to you are a million to one. If you're the one in the million, the odds are no comfort to you at all! However, it just doesn't make any sense to be really scared of something that has a really small chance of happening to you. Nobody can tell you that every flight is safe, or that you'll never be in a car crash, but the odds are with you. (That's more than you can say about gambling, where the odds of winning are *never* with you!)

The other reason you can feel safe in big moving stuff is that the people who make these giant traveling machines are always trying to make them safer. Even though there are more and more cars on the road, and even though they go faster and faster, fewer people are being hurt or killed in cars. Car safety scientists are always thinking up new ways to protect your safety. We just heard of a new kind of car radar that helps drivers see things at night that are way in front of the car, close behind the car, in the blind spots on the sides of the car, or in a spaceship about to come down and land on the car. (It's comforting to know that somebody is protecting you from spaceships landing on your car!) Pretty soon, you might be able to just get in your family's car and tell it to drive you somewhere and then just sit back and let the automatic pilot take over!

The people who make these giant traveling machines are always trying to make them safer.

Airplanes are getting even closer to this kind of technology. There was once a time when airplane pilots couldn't see anything in the dark or in a cloud or in a storm. When Charles Lindbergh flew across the Atlantic Ocean in the year 1927, he had to figure out where to go just by looking out the window. Nowadays a plane can practically take off, show two movies, and land without the pilot doing a thing. Well, that's a big exaggeration—but since computers and satellites tell each other where the plane is, where it should go, what's ahead of it, and what's below it, it's easier for the pilot to make a successful flight.

No computer or air bag can make our travel machines totally safe, but we should feel better knowing that there are lots of people who work every day to figure out how to make the machines we travel in just a little more safe.

Life is full of happy, great things, but life also has dangers.

If we're going to take life's good things, we must also accept life's risks. We can try to lessen the risks and dangers, but we can't make them go away. It's part of the deal we all make to live.

STUFF YOU CAN FIX

People want to get from here to there fast and cheap, and those two things don't always fit together. The faster we travel, the more dangerous it is to us if we crash. And the more people try to get us from here to there cheaply, the more chance there is that they will save money by cutting out something that makes us safe. Safety costs money, and people who run the get-us-from-here-to-there businesses might try to save money so that we can travel cheaply (and so that they can still make money). So we have to keep reminding the get-us-from-here-to-there companies that safety is more important than speed or cheapness. The government helps with this, but grown-ups have to keep reminding the government and the people who make cars and planes that getting there fast is good, and getting there cheaply is good, but getting there safely is by far the most important thing.

One big thing we can fix is to make sure that the people who drive us from here to there are safe drivers. Driving cars or boats or Jet Skis after drinking booze is really dangerous to everybody who is near. Driving too fast, driving while talking on the cell phone, or riding in a car without buckling your seat belt is just not safe—and these very bad habits are also illegal in many places.

SADD (Students Against Drunk Driving) and MADD (Mothers Against Drunk Driving) are two great groups that got started because of the crazy way some kids (and adults) were driving. They started a "designated driver" campaign. When your parents or older siblings are going to a party, somebody should be chosen to be the designated driver. That means that person won't drink alcohol at the party and is responsible for getting everybody home safely.

If your older brother or sister is driving you somewhere while talking on the phone and not paying enough attention to the road, you have the right to say: "Hey, that's not cool. Can't you wait until you're out of the car? I don't wanna end up like chopped liver before soccer practice." (Oh, and don't forget to say, "And besides, I love you and care about your safety!")

Lots of kids think that driver's ed is a joke. We know kids who don't pay attention and goof off in driver's ed class. This is a big mistake. Knowing how to drive safely is a skill you'll need for the rest of your life. And like any other subject, it takes a while to learn. The difference is that not learning algebra won't cause you to smash into a tree and wreck your parents' car—and your life. A car isn't a toy, and learning to drive safely isn't like playing a video game.

Have you ever thought about how powerful a car is? Think about one horse running you over. That could break your back or even kill you. Now think about a hundred or two hundred horses running over you. That's the horsepower of one car. When you become old enough to drive, it's very important for you to respect the power of a car and to drive like you're holding on to two hundred wild horses and not like you're holding on to the handlebars of your bicycle.

We hope that you and your family will never be in danger. But you may know someone someday who has just lost a loved one in a crash. It's hard to know what to say to someone living with a shock like that in their life, but it's important to say *something*. No one expects life-changing words that will take away their grief. They just need to know you care. And that makes all the difference in the world.

Officials

Arrest

No Comfort
In Words
For Victim
Of Abuse

Scho

Video

Man

Teen killed

Ser

chools Show

Jump in Rep

Young V

Abuse

Abuse Charge

sanit crew finds ae

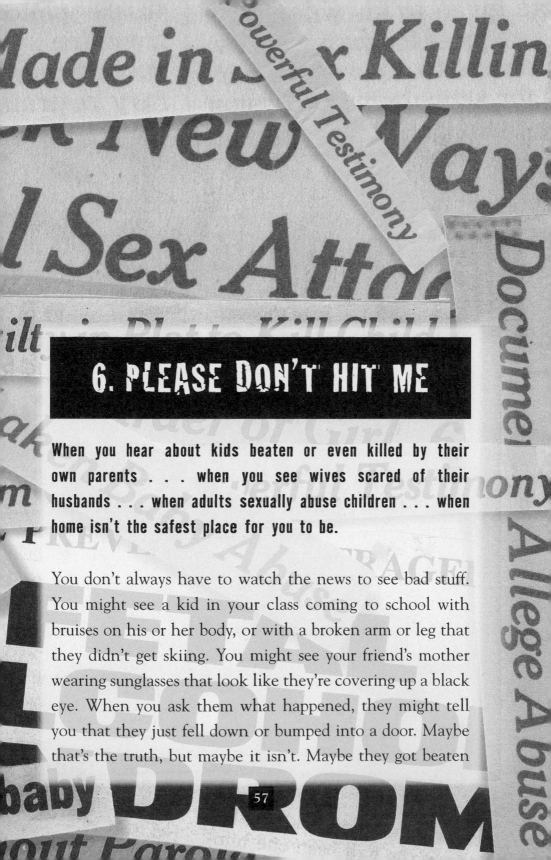

6. PLEASE DON'T HIT ME

When you hear about kids beaten or even killed by their own parents . . . when you see wives scared of their husbands . . . when adults sexually abuse children . . . when home isn't the safest place for you to be.

You don't always have to watch the news to see bad stuff. You might see a kid in your class coming to school with bruises on his or her body, or with a broken arm or leg that they didn't get skiing. You might see your friend's mother wearing sunglasses that look like they're covering up a black eye. When you ask them what happened, they might tell you that they just fell down or bumped into a door. Maybe that's the truth, but maybe it isn't. Maybe they got beaten up by somebody in their family. Most people who get beaten up don't talk about it unless they're forced to, or unless they're desperate and frightened to death.

By the time you see stories of hurting at home on the news, the stories are really bad: kids killed by their moms or dads, or women hunted down by angry husbands or boyfriends. Just getting a black eye or a broken arm isn't a big enough story to get on the news nowadays. You can be sure that every death of every abused adult or kid that you saw on the news came at the end of many days of pain that you never saw. Any murder of any person is a very terrible thing, but when people are killed by their own parents or by their own husband or wife—the people who are supposed to love them more than anyone else—it is much more than a terrible thing. It is a scream-to-the-world-that-this-should-never-happen thing. Our homes should be places of safety, not places of beatings and murder.

We help serve breakfast in a "safe house" every Sunday morning. We're not allowed to give out the address. The women and kids in this house are filled with the deepest fear we have ever seen: They live in fear that their fathers or husbands will suddenly appear and try to hurt them. Usually the women and kids have no money, for many had to run out of the house without taking anything with them. They just want to be safe, like most of us are, but they fear that they never will be. There are just not enough police to personally protect all of the battered wives and children who are running scared.

But it isn't always men who beat or kill kids. Sometimes it's women. And sometimes it's kids' own mothers. These mothers are so angry about being mothers, so angry about being poor, so angry about being left alone to raise their kids, so angry about being alcoholics or drug addicts that they hurt or kill their very own children.

Abuse is the name for this terrible violence against people we're supposed to love. Abuse takes many forms, but all of them leave behind a deeply wounded and frightened human being. Physical abuse, or beating, is just one kind of abuse. Kids and adults can also be abused without ever being hit. This kind of abuse is called verbal abuse, psychological abuse, or mental abuse. It is what happens when somebody is told over and over again, in different ways, that they're no good. It's not when your mom or dad yells at you for not taking out the garbage; it's when they convince you that you *are* the garbage.

If someone is told that he or she is too fat, too dumb, too slow, too ugly, too lazy, or too anything, after a time that person may begin to believe it. Verbal abuse may not seem as bad as physical abuse, but it can be even worse. Being beaten might force a person to get up the courage to move away from the beater or get help. But victims of verbal abuse usually end up staying around and getting more and more abuse. People who are physically hurt may have wounds that call attention to their problem, and friends may offer to help. Verbal abuse doesn't leave a visible bruise, but the inside bruise it leaves is huge. It can destroy a person's self-confidence, and without that, it is very hard to do anything well in life.

Sexual abuse is another form of abuse. If an adult touches your private parts, or makes you do sexual things, or forces you to have sex, it is sexual abuse. Sexual abuse is both physical abuse and terrible mental abuse. We don't understand why some adults are so sick in the head that they want to have sex with kids. Sex is a beautiful way that two married people show their love for each other, and out of that love grows their children who will live on after them. Sex is a form of deep love and trust between adults, and it should never be a way of hurting and violating you.

Many kids who are sexually abused never tell anybody. Sometimes they're just so ashamed and scared that they want to forget it, so they keep it inside. Sometimes it is because the adult sexual abusers threaten to hurt them if they tell. But telling an adult you trust about any kind of abuse is always a good idea. Adults who abuse children will do it again unless they're stopped, and they must be stopped.

STUFF TO UNDERSTAND

There are many reasons why adults physically or verbally abuse kids as well as one another. Sometimes people who feel powerless in their jobs or personal lives try to have power over the people in their own families. Sometimes people who are abused as children grow up to be abusers as adults. Sometimes people who become parents when they're too young and have nobody to help them just can't cope with their responsibilities, and they lash out. Sometimes drugs or alcohol make people violent or abusive. Sometimes people are mentally ill and just can't understand what is real and what isn't real. Whatever the reasons for abuse, these are the things you should understand:

- It *isn't* your fault if your parents are abusing you.
- Nobody *ever* has a right to hurt you!
- You *should* tell some adult you trust if someone is hurting you.
- You *should* tell some adult you trust if someone is hurting your friend.
- There *are* places where you can go to be safe.

We know that when you have a mom and dad who love you and kiss you and give you all the support you need, it's hard to understand how other kids can go to bed afraid of their parents. But if you can try to understand it, you might be able to help a friend who is frightened and feeling alone. Nobody should be beaten behind closed doors and nobody should feel so ashamed or afraid that they lie about it.

STUFF YOU CAN FIX

There are two things that need fixing: the abuser and the abused. You may be able to help one or the other or both, depending on the situation. The abuser needs to face his or her mental illness and learn that causing pain to others is wrong. The abused need to find a safe place to live. Then they need to understand that the abuse was not their fault, and to learn to get back their self-esteem.

Abusers can't get help until they're caught or until they realize that what they're doing is wrong. Doctors and religious counselors can help abusers let go of their anger. It can take a long time, and, to be honest, it doesn't always work. But it can't work at all unless people who see the abuse say something so that the abusers stop hurting and start healing.

Abused people also have a hard journey to healing. Often the person who caused so much pain is a loved one. Sometimes the fear and shame is so great that the abused person just blocks out the memories of the abuse. They force themselves to forget that it ever happened! But we believe that the only good way out of some bad place is *through* it and not around it. Being abused is a bad thing, but it doesn't have to be a secret bad thing. So if you or someone you know has been abused, the best thing you could ever do is to help that person bring all the pain in their life out into the open with the help of a doctor or some other kind of healer.

You can also learn to start protecting yourself. We hope that your mom and dad are great people, and that you never have to fear them. But you can be aware of other dangers. For example, you can't always be sure that the people you meet in a chat room on the Internet are great kids. That neat kid who wants to meet you for lunch someday could really be a creepy man who wants to abuse you. So it's smart not to go into chat rooms with people you don't know.

We know your parents tell you this, but you've gotta believe them on this one—never, ever go anywhere with a stranger. And if an adult you know and thought you trusted asks you to do something scary or weird or if they touch your private parts, it's important to be brave and call the police, your parents, or another grown-up. Most adults love and protect kids, but sadly, not every single one of them does. You have to be smart and careful and protect yourself before you can protect anybody else.

If you see a friend or any kid in school who is beaten up, right away you should tell a grown-up who you trust. They will contact the right people who can try to figure out why that child was hurt and maybe even send a social worker to the family. Sometimes kids hear important stuff that adults don't, so you could be a real help in saving a child who is getting beaten up at home. And if that child is you, please tell somebody that you're hurt and scared. Don't listen to people who tell you to shut up, or the abuse will get worse. You're a special, holy, wonderful person, and nobody has a right to hurt you or tell you that you're dirt. Get away, get safe, and get loved!

We believe that one of the things it means to be a kid is to feel safe and loved. Kids who are abused feel hated and afraid. They may be young, but after they're abused, they're no longer children. Kids deserve time to be kids.

Anti-Sem

Ghosts of Racism Past

Haunting

Present Ar

Woman Sues,
aying Men
Want Her Out

Bias

Races Still Tend to Liv

Racial D

Witnesses Test

Displayed Hatr

nds an I

al Look at Racism Hi

Slave

ssues Surfac

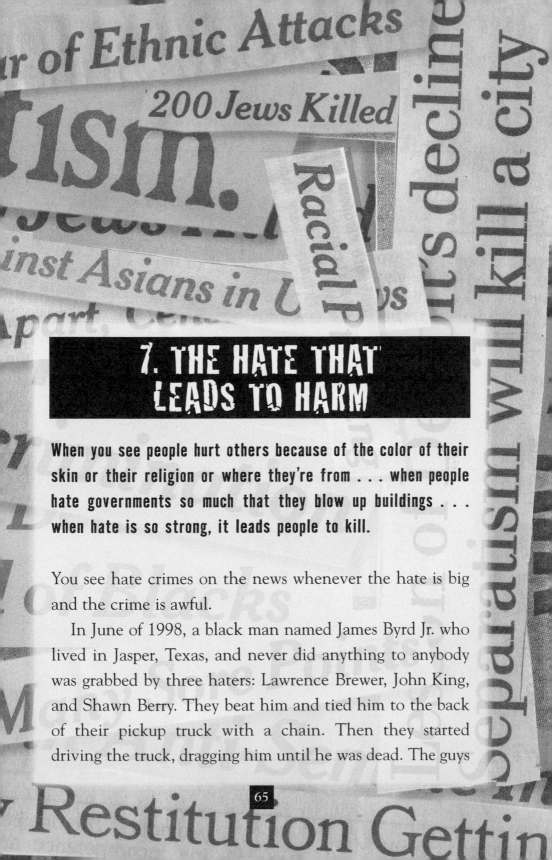

7. THE HATE THAT LEADS TO HARM

When you see people hurt others because of the color of their skin or their religion or where they're from . . . when people hate governments so much that they blow up buildings . . . when hate is so strong, it leads people to kill.

You see hate crimes on the news whenever the hate is big and the crime is awful.

In June of 1998, a black man named James Byrd Jr. who lived in Jasper, Texas, and never did anything to anybody was grabbed by three haters: Lawrence Brewer, John King, and Shawn Berry. They beat him and tied him to the back of their pickup truck with a chain. Then they started driving the truck, dragging him until he was dead. The guys who murdered James Byrd were caught and one of the murderers had a tattoo on his arm showing a black man being hanged from a tree. This is true, terrible racism. Racism is senseless, destructive hatred.

In July of 1999 another hater named Benjamin Nathaniel Smith drove around Illinois shooting blacks and Asians and Jews. He killed two people and injured nine others before he shot himself.

The same year, a man named Buford Furrow came into a Jewish Community Center in Los Angeles where Jewish kids were taken care of, and he started to shoot up the place. He was trying to kill as many Jewish kids as he could. He wounded five people, and then on his way home he killed a mailman who was from the Philippines. When the police caught him the next day in Las Vegas he said, "I did it because I wanted to send a wake-up call to America to kill Jews." This, too, is racism.

When somebody robs a bank or steals a car or sneaks into a baseball game without a ticket, it's bad, but you can understand why they did it. People want stuff without working for it. But when people are beaten or murdered just because of the color of their skin or their religion, it is really hard to understand. It makes no sense to hate someone because they're a woman or a man or because they like women or men or because they or their parents came to this country from another one. How can people hate other people so deeply for such stupid reasons? We're supposed to answer this question for you in this chapter, but we can't do it.

We don't understand hate any better than you do. Hate is foolish and ignorant. But hate lives in the world and on the news, and so somehow we have to try to get rid of this poison for our country, our families, and our insides.

STUFF TO UNDERSTAND

Hate is a feeling, and like all feelings, it can be strong or weak or somewhere in between. The weak form of hate is in lots more people than the strong form of hate. That's the only good thing about hate. The bad part about hate is that if you start out with weak hate, it can get stronger, especially if you have enough haters around you to push you even deeper into hating.

The weakest form of hate can happen when you don't ever really get to know anyone who is very different from you. You might hang around with people just like you, you

> **Hate can happen when you don't ever really get to know anyone who is very different from you.**

might live near people just like you, and you might only join clubs or do things with people just like you. If you ask one of these weak haters if he or she doesn't like people who are different, the answer will probably be no, but the truth is probably yes.

People who are weak haters don't get in much trouble for their hating. One of the reasons that weak haters get away with their hating is that many of the weak haters have money. The more money you have, the more you can choose things that make you comfortable. And human beings are naturally more comfortable with things and with people that are very familiar to them.

A stronger form of hating is when you go from avoiding people who are different from you to showing others that you don't like them. When you're a middle hater, you tell mean jokes about the groups you hate. Or maybe you say bad things about them that are not even jokes. Middle haters actually think that there's something really wrong with the groups they hate. They try to hide their ignorance with made-up reasons to hate people. Middle haters don't hurt the people they hate, but they keep alive the hate and spread the hate to others.

Strong haters are ready to hurt others mentally or physically because of their hate. Strong haters form hate groups that try hard to get weak haters to be middle haters and to get middle haters to be strong haters. They also plan ways to hurt or sometimes even kill the people they hate.

For a long time, hate groups had a very hard time getting people to know about them and getting people to join them. But today, using the Internet, people hiding in their own homes can look up a web site of a hate group and connect with them. We would never tell you the names of these hate groups, because we don't want to give them any more publicity that might help them spread their poison. The people who murdered James Byrd were trying to start a hate group, and their horrible crime was a sick way to get other haters to know about their group.

As hard as it is to understand hate, people have tried to explain this deep and awful human emotion. Some believe that haters use their hate to make themselves feel powerful when they really feel weak and powerless. By hating other people, the hater feels that he or she is better than somebody else. If someone is poor or with little or no education or has a lousy job or is lonely with no real friends, joining a hate group might offer that person "friends" who will hate along with him or her—and a place to feel a part of something powerful and big.

Some people think haters got their poison from their parents. In some homes, hatred is a part of the family's beliefs. When hatred comes from loved ones, it's very hard to know that it's hatred. It just seems natural and normal, but it's not. Healthy families teach people about love and compassion, not hatred and violence.

STUFF YOU CAN FIX

Hatred is like acid in your soul and in your life. It eats away at the best parts of you and replaces them with a stinking mess. After hating for many years, a hater can't live without hate, because it's all that's left inside. So getting rid of your own hatred—even if it's weak hatred—isn't only good for the people you hate. It's also good for you. It's like taking your insides to a car wash and cleaning out all the crud that got stuck between the seats.

Before you can fix hate in the world, you have to fix it in yourself. Of all the bad stuff you see on the news, hatred is one thing you really *can* fix in a small but important way. All of us have some hatred in us (except for a few really *unbelievably* good people), and we have to try to find those hatreds and let them go. Maybe you grew up in a place that just didn't have many Latinos, Asians, or some other ethnic group, so you didn't know much about them. Maybe you heard jokes about them that made you form opinions about these people that were unfair. When you don't know anybody from another race or culture, fear of the unknown makes it hard to keep out hatred and prejudice.

The more you learn about other kinds of people, the harder it will be for you to hate.

So one big good thing to do would be to try to get to know the people you know nothing about. Eat lunch with different kinds of kids at school. Trade your peanut butter sandwich for a sushi roll! Try to read stories about other cultures. Go to other places of worship to learn about how they love God. The more you learn about other kinds of people, the harder it will be for you to hate. When somebody tells a joke that puts down another group of people, don't laugh. You can even tell them that the joke is *not* funny to you.

A few months before we wrote this book, some haters smeared paint on synagogues and churches in Oceanside, Long Island, a town near us. People were very upset to see signs of hate in their town, but what they did next was just great. They didn't just let the police handle everything. Instead, they held a rally in the high school auditorium and asked us and other grown-ups to come and speak. Speaker after speaker stood up and said that hatred had no place in Oceanside. The feeling of unity and hope we all felt that day drove out the hate. The kids who did the crime were found, and the community was stronger than it had ever been.

In Montana one winter not so long ago, some haters saw a Chanukah menorah in the window of a Jewish family. They threw a brick through their window and scared them terribly. The next day, a local minister made paper menorahs for all the families of his church and they all put the menorahs in their windows. It was a beautiful sign that hatred was not welcome in that town and in their hearts.

There's an old story about why God made just one person at the very beginning of creation (the way it's told in the Bible, anyway). God said, "I made just one person at first so that in the times to come, nobody would ever be able to say, 'My ancestor was greater than yours.' "

We may all have Adam in our family, but we often forget. Someday maybe we will live knowing that our family includes all people everywhere.

but A

Scoreb rd

Scoreb

Som

Season

Bruis

Dozens Crus

SP EL

ORTS

s, Aghast at Risks, Want Ru

ou

Hu
N

Don't Play It Safe, and Pay Price

CORECE

OE HATRE

Blood on Ice, but Anoth

ictory on

Cente

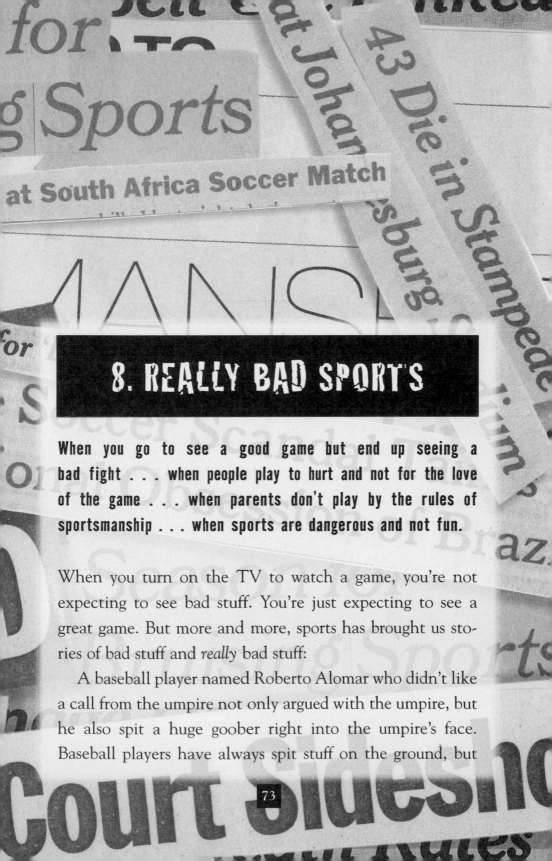

8. REALLY BAD SPORTS

When you go to see a good game but end up seeing a bad fight . . . when people play to hurt and not for the love of the game . . . when parents don't play by the rules of sportsmanship . . . when sports are dangerous and not fun.

When you turn on the TV to watch a game, you're not expecting to see bad stuff. You're just expecting to see a great game. But more and more, sports has brought us stories of bad stuff and *really* bad stuff:

A baseball player named Roberto Alomar who didn't like a call from the umpire not only argued with the umpire, but he also spit a huge goober right into the umpire's face. Baseball players have always spit stuff on the ground, but now the umpires' faces are getting in the way of the spit! Then a pitcher named Roger Clemens threw a sharp piece of broken bat toward Mike Piazza during the 2000 World Series. (Some people thought if there had been a chair and some pots and pans on the mound, Clemens might have thrown them, too!) There's just no reason for baseball to get disgusting or violent.

The boxer Mike Tyson bit off a part of Evander Holyfield's ear during their championship heavyweight fight in 1997. Some people think that boxing is already too violent a sport, but nobody thinks that boxing should allow ear biting! Even in a normally peaceful game like tennis, players like John McEnroe have argued and sworn at umpires, line judges, and fans in the crowd when they didn't like a call.

Some people think that hockey is being ruined by so many fights. There are too many players who hurt players on the opposing team. Marty McSorley once snuck up behind Donald Brashear and whacked him hard in the head. Brashear went to the hospital and his injuries could have been fatal. In pro football, a whole bunch of players have almost been killed by other players who may have cared about winning more than the safety of the other players.

The wrestling shows we see on television are all about violence. They're not real. The people who put them on decide who will win and who will lose, which means they're "fixed." But even if it is pretend, the violence in wrestling is really dangerous. Not long ago, a kid in Florida killed a little girl by smashing her around in the same way he saw on a wrestling show. And her death was not fake and not fixed—it was tragic.

Sometimes the bad news in sports comes from the fans and not from the players:

Every year there's at least one story about a huge riot at a soccer game somewhere in the world where fans are trampled to death. Some people are even killed in fights with fans of the other team. There are now soccer stadiums with cages around the fans that keep them from throwing things at the players.

Many baseball parks don't sell beer after the seventh inning anymore because fans were getting drunk, throwing things on the field, or starting fights with other fans. Police have said that the most violence in homes happens after a football game when the home team has lost. And if the home team in any sport *wins* a world championship, you can pretty much bet that after the game, some crazy fans will turn over cars, break store windows, start fires, and act like wild dogs as their sick way of celebrating.

Believe it or not, some grown-ups can't even behave at *kids'* sports events. Not long before we wrote this book, there was a news story about a soccer game in New Jersey that had to be stopped by police because of a huge fight between the parents. The soccer game was for eight-year-old girls! We also heard a terrible story on national TV about a dad who killed another dad (who was on the ice supervising a hockey game) because he didn't think the right calls were being made. One of the saddest parts about the bad stuff in sports is when parents can't protect their kids from bad sportsmanship, and when parents turn into bad sports themselves.

If parents can't be good sports, how can kids? Kids playing tennis argue line calls more and more. Fights break out in kids' baseball and football all the time. Some coaches teach kids how to "get tough," but what they really mean is "play dirty." Bad sportsmanship is when a person forgets how to play the game in a respectful way. Bad sportsmanship is one of the small but very real bad things in the news, and it is everywhere.

STUFF TO UNDERSTAND

Sports is not life, but sports is like life. In sports, as in life, you have to learn how to keep trying, how to learn from your defeats, and how to win graciously. In sports, like life, you're going to find people who just never learned to play by the rules, and you'll have to decide how you're going to handle them. In sports and in life, there's lots of pressure to win. How we deal with that pressure is our choice. The choices we make will shape us into a person everyone respects—or maybe they will turn us into a liar or a cheat who will do anything to win.

The pressures to win can sometimes come from the people you love the most. Some parents want their kids to win in sports so badly that they make their kids nuts. Maybe the parents are trying to live their own dreams through their kids. Maybe they hope their child can get a sports scholarship so they won't have to spend so much money to send their child to college. Maybe they feel it's important to have something to brag to their friends about at dinner parties. All this pressure turns sports into a job. It changes the reason for playing from loving the game to loving money and fame.

Drug use is another result of the pressure in sports to win. Many professional athletes take drugs called steroids to make them stronger and faster and tougher. Even high school athletes are taking performance drugs to make them play better. But these drugs can also hurt their bodies, sometimes even fatally. So real athletes don't need help from drugs—they count on their own training and determination. Still, drugs are everywhere in sports and they're everywhere in life.

STUFF YOU CAN FIX

Good people are good sports. If sports doesn't make you better and make your life better, then sports are a joke. Sports are supposed to be fun and keep our bodies in shape. Sports are supposed to make us keep trying to get better at things we're good at. Sports are supposed to show us how to be a part of a team. Sports are supposed to teach us to live by the rules. Sports are supposed to help us to learn how to lose, not just how to win. If playing sports ever becomes nothing but pressure and fighting and cheating and fear and drugs and money, it is no longer sports. It has become a sick and twisted thing.

The bad stuff in sports is bad stuff that you can really *do* something about as a kid. You can teach others to be good sports just by your own example. It's normal to get frustrated when you or your teammates are making the same mistakes over and over, but everyone knows that yelling and cursing doesn't make anything better. When people yell at you, does it make it any easier for you to hit the ball or make the goal? It probably makes it *harder*! So if you want a teammate who keeps messing up to get better, the best thing to do would be to talk to the kid after the game and tell him or her not to feel bad about what happened. And you can offer to practice with them sometime or offer tips on what might help.

More important than focusing on what went wrong in a game is thinking about what went right. What did you do well? What did the team do well? You'll find sports are a whole lot more fun when you look on the bright side. That doesn't mean you shouldn't think about what went wrong in order to do better next time, but first and foremost, remember the good stuff. And remember to have fun.

If you love sports, you should find some time to think about how you play and why you play. If your parents are making you nuts about winning or if they're acting like nuts when they come to see your games, maybe it's time for you to talk to them about how you're feeling. Maybe they're doing all this bad stuff because they love you and they think they're helping you become a stronger person. But if you tell them that they're *not* helping you at all, maybe they will change the way they act. If you don't say anything, nothing will change.

It may not be your job to change how professional athletes act, but one thing you can do is choose sports heroes who are good people. Some athletes say that kids don't look to them as role models in life, but that's stupid. Sports stars are heroes for lots of kids, and sports stars should try to live their lives in a way that will make their fans proud of them. If they don't, they don't deserve to have fans. Being good at sports and being good are just not the same thing.

There are lots of athletes who are great human beings. Dikembe Mutombo is not only a great basketball player, he's also building hospitals in Nigeria. Tiger Woods gives away lots of his money to help poor kids get clubs and learn golf. Pat LaFontaine, one of the greatest hockey players of all time, collected stories about great athletes who are also great people. These people are generous with their time, money, and talent, and so they're heroes.

Sometimes the greatest champions are not on television, but right next door or in your very own home. Recently we were watching physically challenged kids compete in a sports event near where we live—kids in wheelchairs and on crutches, kids with diseases that twisted their bones, kids with brain problems. The field where all these kids came to run, jump, and roll in their races was the exact place where Charles Lindbergh took off in his plane to be the first person to fly alone across the Atlantic Ocean. It reminded us that heroes and great accomplishments come in all shapes and sizes.

oil on

climate

Foes of New Generators
Say Pollution Is Likely

DEA

OR

More Rolling Blackouts

ALIV

Economic boon,
environmental disruption—
Alaska weighs the problem

Bush Reverses

Gas Tied to Glob

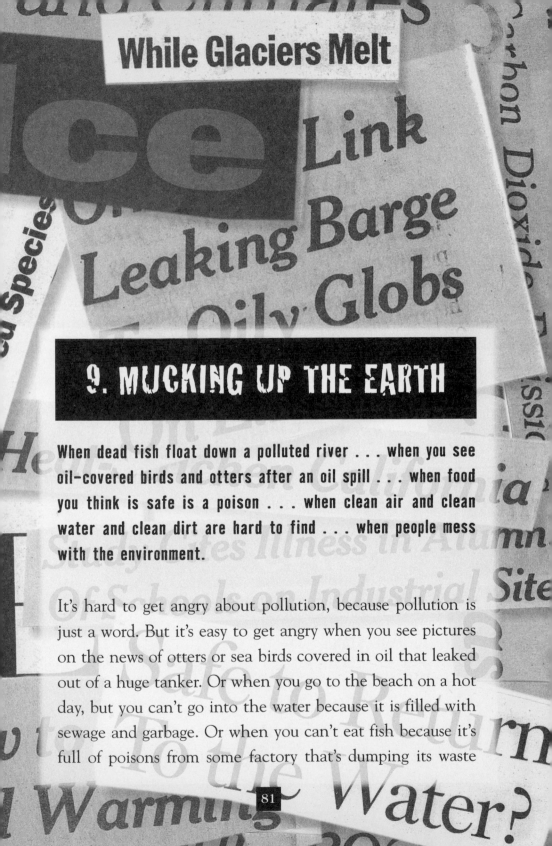

While Glaciers Melt

Ice

Link

Leaking Barge

Oily Globs

9. MUCKING UP THE EARTH

When dead fish float down a polluted river . . . when you see
oil-covered birds and otters after an oil spill . . . when food
you think is safe is a poison . . . when clean air and clean
water and clean dirt are hard to find . . . when people mess
with the environment.

It's hard to get angry about pollution, because pollution is
just a word. But it's easy to get angry when you see pictures
on the news of otters or sea birds covered in oil that leaked
out of a huge tanker. Or when you go to the beach on a hot
day, but you can't go into the water because it is filled with
sewage and garbage. Or when you can't eat fish because it's
full of poisons from some factory that's dumping its waste

into a river. Or when you see cities covered with smog so thick that it's amazing people can even breathe. Or when you learn about a cute animal that has just been declared extinct because humans have destroyed its natural habitat. These pictures give pollution and environmental destruction a real face and make them much more than words. They help us to get angry about the way our world is being filled with crud.

Some people think that the worst problem coming from pollution is invisible to most of us right now. It's called global warming, and it happens because the smoke from all the cars, trucks, factories, and power plants puts stuff into the air that traps heat, making the overall temperature on our planet warmer. This heat melts ice at the North and South Poles, which could cause very bad weather and flooding all over the earth so that maybe someday Florida will be under water and Ohio will be on the coast of the Atlantic Ocean. Global warming could also cause drought and famine in other places. It's hard to believe that pollution could change the weather all over the earth, but that's exactly what's happening.

STUFF TO UNDERSTAND

Most pollution doesn't come from bad people who want to muck up the earth. Pollution really comes from all of us who want cheap electricity and cheap gas and cheap things that make our lives easier and more comfortable. Most of us don't care how the stuff we want gets to be cheap—or else we don't understand it. Here are some examples of how the way we live our lives every day causes pollution:

We want to drive our cars wherever we go. We don't like using buses or trains or car pools because we don't like to be crowded, don't want to wait around for other people, and we like to listen to our own music very loud. We love big cars that use a lot of gas but look cool and hold lots of stuff so we don't get bored on our family trips.

Now, to be able to get cheap gas to drive our big cars wherever we want to go whenever we want to get there, we need oil, lots of oil, gobs of oil to turn into gasoline. Most of the oil we use comes from lands far away, and it's sent here in oil tankers. If you sent oil in small oil tankers, the chances of a big oil spill would be small because there isn't that much oil on each ship, but it's more expensive to send oil this way. The cheapest way is to send gigantic oil tankers that hold millions of gallons. But if just one of these starts leaking, there can be a huge oil spill.

Of all the gasoline made on planet earth, most of it is used right here in America, even though most of the people on planet earth don't live in America. Getting more oil and natural gas to run our cars and machines means drilling more holes in the earth to pull it out. Some of the places where the oil and gas are buried are very wild, filled with animals that have never seen a truck. Drilling in those places may force the animals to leave their homes. Oil can also be found in the ocean floor. But if the oil drilling platforms—just offshore from some of our biggest cities and nicest beaches—were to break in a storm, we'd have dead oily birds up and down our coastlines.

If we decide to buy oil from other countries, we have no choice but to pay whatever price they ask. That means we have to pay more for almost everything. So getting more oil means making choices, and all the choices seem pretty bad. If the oil companies asked most people if they would pay more money for gasoline to keep down the danger of oil spills or to avoid drilling in new areas, most people would go for the cheap gas and the oily birds. If cleaning up the earth costs more money at the gas pump, lots of people decide not to care about the earth as much as they care about cheap gas, plastics, jet fuel, and all of the other cool stuff you can make out of oil.

Another cause of pollution is our need for electricity. So many things we have use up electricity that it is hard for the electric companies to keep up with our needs: computers, televisions and video games, radios and CD players, lights, air conditioners, microwave ovens, dishwashers, vacuums, and hair dryers—all of these things and much, much more use up electricity. The year we wrote this book, California had to turn off or turn down the electricity all over the state at different times because they didn't have enough for everyone all of the time. There's talk about building more power plants to generate more electricity. But the more power plants we build, the more smoke stacks we'll have that put bad stuff into the air. So getting more electricity usually means getting more pollution.

Some people think that the answer is to find ways to use lots less energy. The word for this is conservation. Another answer is to create machines that don't need so much gasoline and oil and natural gas. People are also exploring other ways to generate electricity that don't put bad stuff into the air. This is called alternative energy. There are solar panels that turn sunlight into electricity. There are windmills that turn wind into electricity. There are hydroelectric plants that turn running river water into electricity. There are even methane plants in garbage dumps that turn the macaroni and cheese you ate last month for dinner into electricity. There are cars that run on batteries with just a little gasoline that can go 100 miles on a single gallon of gas.

The problem is that the new ways to get power all cost more than oil, and it is really hard to get people to pay more money for something they could get for less. Also some of the newer ways to get power are not considered reliable. Batteries are heavy and expensive and they pollute the earth when you bury them, and there's not enough macaroni and cheese to run anything. Finding new ways to get energy that don't cost an arm and a leg, that don't coat animals with oil or destroy our wild places, and that don't mess up the air or the water is one of the really great problems of the world.

STUFF YOU CAN FIX

You may think that there's nothing you can do to fix a problem as big as pollution, but there really is lots you can do.

These things will not end pollution, but they may lower pollution in your corner of planet earth, which is all anybody
could expect from you, seeing as how you're just a kid.

One big thing you can do is recycle. Lots of people are
into recycling nowadays, and maybe you're already doing it.
You can set up different trash cans in your house: one for
paper, one for glass, one for aluminum, one for plastic, and
one for macaroni. Each town has its own way of collecting
and sorting this garbage. In some places you can even make
money turning in old soda cans or bottles. Recycling helps
with the pollution problem in two ways. When the people
who make soda cans make new ones, they don't need to dig
for as much new aluminum ore in the earth. The people who
make paper don't need to cut down as many new trees. The
people who make plastic bottles don't have to use so much
oil and chemicals (that's right—plastic comes from oil).
And we don't have to ruin beautiful lands and animal habi-
tats by turning them into waste dumps. Recycling helps.

Another way to fix the problem of pollution is to turn off
the lights when you leave a room, don't let the water run
when you're brushing your teeth, and don't throw the towel
into the hamper after only using it once, to name just a few.
At school, you can write a report on pollution and
the environment, and think up fun ways to help conserve
energy with your friends and teachers. You can recycle the
stuff you use at school. You could probably come up with
even better ideas on your own. Some of the biggest ideas
come from the smallest people.

As a family, there's lots you can do. You can ask your parents to turn the air-conditioning off when it's not boiling hot outside or to turn the heat down when it's not totally freezing outside so that you can save electricity. Keeping your house a little warmer in the summer and a little colder in the winter saves energy and is one important way that you and your family can help to reduce the number of dead oily birds in the world. And by the way, conserving energy will also save your family money on energy bills (and you can use the extra money to buy more macaroni and cheese).

If your parents allow it and you're old enough, you might try walking or biking to your sports practice, to your piano lesson, or to your friend's house, depending on where you live. We have gotten so used to being driven everywhere, we've forgotten how much every little bit of driving affects our environment. And when it's time to buy a new car, maybe your family will think about buying a smaller car that uses less gas. Maybe you can tell your parents that you don't have to buy the monster SUV (Sport Utility Vehicle) that weighs almost three tons and sucks a lot of gas. Everyone got around just fine before we had giant cars!

The biggest thing you can do to fix pollution is to believe a simple idea: LESS IS MORE. Having more stuff and using up more stuff is not as good as living a little more simply and a little less selfishly. Less is more means that all of us could live with less food, less paper, less electricity, and less stuff. And if each of us uses less, the world will have more—and there will be more of this beautiful planet to share in the future.

ed Cocaine Lord Is Arre

THE PREVENTABL

Glitter Hides Dark Side of Young

Violent Crime

Marijuana's Me

Unwinnable War on Drugs

Yank faces new
Russian drug charges

10. SAD & SCARY ADDICTS

When you see famous people ruined by drugs . . . when you see ordinary people killed by drunk drivers . . . when drug dealers shoot people and get shot . . . when people think that they need chemicals to be happy.

You would be amazed at how much bad stuff in the news comes from drugs and booze. People rob and steal and beat up and shoot and kill to get drugs and drug money. Drug dealers have paid money to cops and politicians to leave them alone and let them bring drugs into this country. Famous actors, rock stars, and sports figures are always on the front pages of newspapers for getting busted for drug use, and often drug addiction ruins their careers. And time and

time again, drugs kill the people who take them by destroy-
ing their bodies and their brains slowly or fast, depending on
how much and what kind of drugs they use.

There are expensive, harder-to-get drugs that make the
news, like heroin or ecstasy or cocaine, but legal drugs are
all around us, too. Some kids do "huffing"—sniffing glue or
the stuff in spray cans—because it gets them high, but it can
also kill them.

Another drug that's everywhere is nicotine, which gets
into you when you smoke cigarettes. Kids who smoke don't
think they're doing drugs. But nicotine can be just as addictive as heroin and just as hard a habit to kick. Every day
3,000 kids smoke their first cigarette because they think
that smoking makes you look cool. But what they're forget-

Kids who smoke don't think they're doing drugs.

ting is that once you're hooked, smoking can cause lung
cancer, breathing problems, and other health problems. It's
one of the sneakiest and deadliest things you might normally face as a kid. Getting some heroin may be difficult and
dangerous, but getting a cigarette is easy and dangerous.

Alcohol is the most common drug because it is legal for
adults over twenty-one. You probably don't think of alcohol
as a drug, but it is, and it's involved in a lot of the bad stuff
in the news. Alcohol can cause violence in the home and

tragic car crashes on the road. Alcohol is often an influence in sexual crimes, when drunk men try to force women to have sex with them. And at colleges and universities, where drinking is often part of the scene, every year there's a sad story about a kid who went to a party and drank so much alcohol in such a short period of time that he or she died of alcohol poisoning.

Like other types of drugs, alcohol can be addictive. Too much alcohol too much of the time can make people lose touch with the real world. An alcoholic might lose a job, flunk out of school, or have relationship problems with friends and family. You don't hear a lot about this in the news, because sadly, it's so common and so hidden. Addiction and the many other problems that come along with it happen to families all over America, every day. Your next-door neighbors may be struggling with it, and you might not even know it. But if you *have* been unlucky enough to see what addiction can do to a person and to a family, you know how very difficult it is to heal the inside and outside pain it can cause.

STUFF TO UNDERSTAND

Addiction is a scary thing because if you're an addict, you don't have much control over your own body. Something more powerful begins to take charge. Addiction is a trap that takes you in by making you feel terrific for a few hours, but then traps you into coming back again and again to get high or get drunk. Addiction keeps you using drugs or drink-ing alcohol even though you know you should stop, even if you're *trying* to stop. Your body and mind crave the drug like it is food or water they need to stay alive. That's why addic-tion is so hard to break. Getting addicted takes a short time, but getting healed takes a long time.

Getting addicted takes a short time, but getting healed takes a long time.

Addiction is a sickness, and addicts need doctors to help them get well. They need doctors and substance abuse counselors to care for them while their body gets used to working without drugs in a hospital or drug rehab center. Then they need doctors and counselors to help them stay clean when they leave. Rehab can mean over a year of being away from the normal world. With support from friends and family, addicts *can* recover, but there's no guarantee.

Even though addiction is an illness, it isn't like most other illnesses, because it only happens if we make bad choices. Other illnesses like the flu or even cancer can hap-pen to us no matter what we do. You don't become a drug addict or an alcoholic because of some germ that flies through the air and lands on you and makes you a junkie or a drunk. You become an alcoholic or a drug addict only one way: when you decide to use stuff that you know can kill because you want to get high or drunk, because you want to look cool, or because you want to escape some inside pain. So the way the sickness enters our bodies and our lives is both our choice and our fault.

Sometimes we get away with the bad choice. Not everybody who ever uses drugs becomes an addict. But every addict started out using just a little. Then the little got so big that they lost the way back to good health and good choices.

> **Every addict started out using just a little.**

One way that people go from being casual users of drugs and social drinkers to being drug addicts and alcoholics is that they don't see the link between what happens at their friends' parties and the bad drug stories they see on the news. Someday, you might find yourself at a party where some kids you know are doing drugs or drinking because they say it is fun and cool. You know that they're not addicts or drug dealers, so you might say, "All right, I'll give it a try. It doesn't seem to have hurt them. It won't hurt me." And if the kids offering you drugs and booze are popular, or if they're your friends, you might feel lots of pressure to join them. After a few parties and before you understand what has happened to you, you're lost in the fog. Like every roller coaster, it starts slowly, but by the end of the ride you're screaming.

> **Inside pain doesn't go away unless you find it, understand it, and figure out a way to let it go.**

Some people use drugs and alcohol not because they tried it for fun at a party where their friends told them that it's a cool thing to do. Some people use drugs to cover up inside pain. Inside pain isn't like the pain you feel when you break a leg. That's outside pain. Your body usually heals and gets rid of outside pain. But inside pain doesn't go away unless you find it, understand it, and figure out a way to let it go. Inside pain is worse than outside pain because it is harder to find and harder to heal.

The inside pain that turns some people to drugs or booze is often a feeling of loneliness, that they don't have the love they need; or sometimes it's too much pressure from others or ourselves to do well and be the best; or sometimes it's just confusion about where our lives are going. Drugs and booze offer a quick patch to cover the inside pain caused by these problems. They send chemicals to the brain that trick the brain into feeling happy for just a little while. But when the drug wears off, the inside pain returns even worse than before.

Most addicts in this world are just normal people like you and us (that is, if you consider us normal!). Addicts are not freaks, even though sometimes drug or alcohol abuse can turn them into something scary and freaky. They just did something that's frighteningly easy for anyone to do: They ended up making a very bad choice by turning to drugs. If you're reading this book, we're pretty sure you'll never make the wrong choice of turning to drugs. But that doesn't mean you'll never be affected by the problem if someone in your family or a friend makes that bad choice.

Alcoholism and drug addiction is a family problem, not just one person's problem. The best way to get well is for the people who love you to help you get well. That support and strength is the best medicine to fight addiction. The problem is that many families ignore the signs so they don't have to deal with what's happening. Helping drug addicts usually means getting tough with them. The love they need isn't always gentle and soft. Sometimes love means saying: "You're sick and I'm not going to let you kill yourself. I love you too much to let you do what you want because what you want is not what you need." We get sick as a family and we can usually only get well as a family.

If you know someone—a friend or a family member—who is addicted to drugs or alcohol, it's important to know that you can't fix this huge problem all by yourself. You need the help of adults and professionals, so you should start by talking to someone older whom you trust.

STUFF YOU CAN FIX

People talk a lot about the drug war we see on television, which is something like this: Soldiers try to find the places where drugs are made and destroy them, while the police try to find and bust the drug dealers. What doesn't get on the news is the one sure way to win the drug war, and that's to lower the number of people who want to buy drugs. If fewer people use drugs, fewer people will sell drugs and fewer people will make drugs. It is the hardest thing to fix but it is the only real fix for this problem. And it has to start with you making good choices!

The things you can fix are easy to say but hard to do. We know that it is hard to say no to things that look fun and cool, but part of growing up is learning how to make choices that will give you the best life in the future. Our mothers had a saying that you may have heard from your own mother: "If your friends were all going to jump off a bridge, would you do it, too?" Learning how to do what is good for us and right for the world is sometimes hard, but always worth it. It is the learning that makes you grow up good and not just tall.

If you grow up tempted to get away from the real world by drinking or doing drugs, you might have inside pain that

Learning how to do what is good for us and right for the world is sometimes hard, but always worth it.

you're trying to get away from. The best way and the only way to deal with inside pain is to talk about it—maybe first with a friend or loved one or grown-up whom you trust, but more importantly with a doctor or some other professional counselor who will work with you to help you understand what has made you hurt inside. Maybe they will talk to you and help you figure out what's going on in your life, or maybe they will give you medicine that can change your feelings without getting you addicted to illegal drugs. Any option is better than letting your inside pain lead you to hurt yourself and others through drugs or alcohol. Drugs and booze cause more pain than they hide.

We believe you can do the right thing. We believe you can be a healthy you. Just try real hard, choose good friends, and most of all . . . choose life.

MISSING MEMORIES

When does Alzheimer's disease begin? A study suggests the damage starts earlier than you think

Parkins...

As Fetal C...

AIDS DRUG BATTL... DEEPENS IN AFR...

Untreated jau... to brain damag...

...S EBOL... ...K LIKE CHICK...

Meningitis Spr...

...CANN Does ... THE PATH

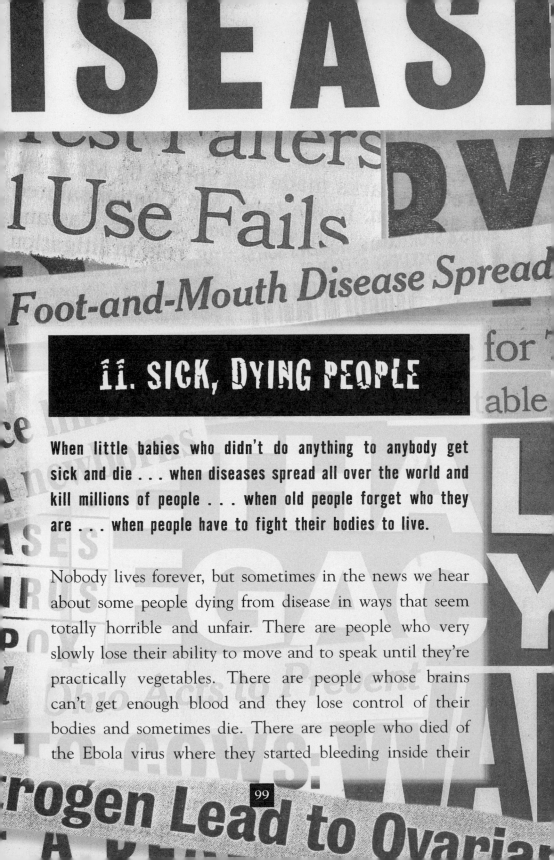

11. SICK, DYING PEOPLE

When little babies who didn't do anything to anybody get sick and die . . . when diseases spread all over the world and kill millions of people . . . when old people forget who they are . . . when people have to fight their bodies to live.

Nobody lives forever, but sometimes in the news we hear about some people dying from disease in ways that seem totally horrible and unfair. There are people who very slowly lose their ability to move and to speak until they're practically vegetables. There are people whose brains can't get enough blood and they lose control of their bodies and sometimes die. There are people who died of the Ebola virus where they started bleeding inside their bodies and then outside from their eyes, nose, and mouth.

To get on the news, a sickness has to be really big or really gross or really scary. An illness that has spread very fast to a lot of people by infection is called an epidemic. The news cares about epidemics, because people are always afraid that an epidemic might spread to their own neighborhoods. The epidemics the news cares most about are the ones that have killed a lot of people. Behind all those big numbers, though, are real human beings who suffer and die and don't have a chance to see tomorrow's sunrise.

> **Behind all those big numbers are real human beings who suffer and die and don't have a chance to see tomorrow's sunrise.**

The epidemics you might see on the news nowadays are often more common in developing countries where hunger and poverty are very big problems. Cholera, diphtheria, dysentery, parasites, malnutrition, and many other diseases all come from not having enough good food or clean water or clean places to get out of the sun or rain.

Some epidemics are happening right in our backyards. When we wrote this book, the most talked about epidemic in the world was AIDS (Acquired Immune Deficiency Syndrome). This means that one of the most important systems in the body, the system that works to fight bad germs in our bodies and that makes us well when we're sick, no longer works right. A body becomes horribly worn down by bad germs because it can't fight them off. A common cold could kill someone with AIDS. Having no defense against illness is a very scary thought.

In America, hundreds of thousands of people have AIDS. In Africa, if you randomly picked any four people, the short odds are that one of them has AIDS or will get it in his or her lifetime. There are medicines that can slow down the damage AIDS does to the body, but these medicines are very expensive to buy and many of the people with AIDS in Africa and around the world can't afford them.

Other diseases have been on the news recently, too. Mad cow disease mostly just kills cows, but it can also infect people who eat meat from a sick cow. It's hard not to be scared of mad cow disease when you see those pictures on the news of a sick cow shaking and trembling uncontrollably. West Nile virus is a disease that's carried by mosquitoes. If a mosquito carrying the virus bites a person, the person could get sick and even die. The hantavirus comes from mouse poop, and it also can kill.

These are diseases you hear about in the news, but the number of people who have actually gotten them and died from them is actually pretty small. But people are terrified when things they thought were no big deal (like a mosquito bite or mouse poop or eating beef) or good and trustworthy (like your immune system) suddenly become a threat. And fear makes for good TV ratings during news time.

There are other kinds of disease scares in the news. We heard a lot about a very popular restaurant near us where 500 people got sick from shish kebabs containing *E. coli* bacteria. It's true that if a waiter or cook in a restaurant where you're eating doesn't wash his or her hands after going to the bathroom and then touches your food, you could get sick from *E. coli* or salmonella. (So you probably want to remember to wash your own hands before you touch your food, too!) Lately we've also seen news reporters going around doing secret testing in delis, restaurants, and other places where food is sold, and then telling everyone watching the show where "bad stuff" like *E. coli* is found in the food.

Even though people still worry like crazy about disease today, in the past diseases were much worse and much more common. They were a part of everyone's life! About 700

> In the past, diseases were much worse and much more common.

years ago, an epidemic of cholera killed one out of every three people in Europe. When European explorers came to areas that we now know as Latin America and the

Caribbean, they brought diseases from Europe like chicken pox and smallpox, killing millions of the native people who lived here. Without modern medicine, diseases which do not worry us much today were often life-threatening. Many children never had a chance to grow up, and women could die during childbirth. We are lucky that we don't have to worry so much about these things today.

Not so long ago, when we were growing up, people worried about a disease called polio, which killed a lot of people and crippled thousands more until a vaccine was discovered. Today we all hope and pray that somebody will find a vaccine for AIDS and that this epidemic will also end. Tom's brother, Gerry, died of AIDS, which was a terrible tragedy for him and his whole family. We pray that pretty soon this won't happen to anyone else. Because even if a disease kills just one person and that person is someone you love, then in your life it *feels* as big and bad as an epidemic.

STUFF TO UNDERSTAND

One of the best ways to not be scared of horrible diseases is to learn more about them. Most of the time, you discover that either the disease you're scared of is much more difficult to get that you had imagined, or that there are treatments that can help or are being developed for that disease. Or, if the disease is a more common one, perhaps there are normal and reasonable safety steps you can take to prevent catching a disease you're afraid of. Either way, the odds are very long that you'll catch some strange disease and die at a young age!

Still, it's important to accept that everyone dies someday, and most people die of some disease. Even if you're lucky and take care of yourself and live to be 100 years old, your body is going to wear out and get weak and get sick and just give out all together. That's just the way it is when you're a human being living on planet earth. Diseases are a part of Nature and we are a part of Nature.

In the chapter about disasters, we talked about how Nature lives and breathes, and sometimes we just have to get out of the way. Disease is a little bit like that.

Some disease happens when certain parts of Nature get mixed up with parts of a person that it shouldn't get mixed up in. A type of germ or bacteria that does good things for life in one place doesn't necessarily do good things when it gets into the wrong place in you.

Other kinds of disease happen when humans mess around with Nature and Nature doesn't like it. When man-made chemicals seep into the soil or into the air or water and then tumors start growing in humans, it's Nature's way of telling us we have to be careful what we do, and that Nature will always be more powerful than we are. Nature likes itself the way God gave it to us and doesn't like it when we upset its balance.

Sometimes the choices we make can determine what makes us sick. When people smoke their whole life and then get lung cancer, their bad choice helped to make them sick. When people eat too much junk food, or when they work too much and rest too little, they're more likely to get heart disease. It was their unhealthy choices that probably made them sick, not a germ floating in the air, a mosquito bite, or some mouse poop. That doesn't mean people who make bad choices *deserve* to get sick; it just means learning to make good choices in your own life is very important. And while good choices can't guarantee perfect health, making bad choices can really shorten the odds of getting very sick.

STUFF YOU CAN FIX

When someone is really sick, the only good thing about it is that all the people who love the sick person get a chance to help him or her. Even if you can't cure a disease, you can cure a big part of a sick person by giving him or her hope and love and care. Love is great medicine. We have heard about studies done that have shown

Love is great medicine.

signs that laughter, hope (what we call *optimism*), and even prayer can truly make a person well! So when you hear that somebody you know or love is sick, call them, visit them, or do what you can to make their life just a little bit easier. It sounds hard, but it's not. Most sick people just want company, and to talk about normal stuff like music, movies, sports, or that goofy dream you had last night.

There will never be a time on earth when there are no diseases. But there will also never be a time when people aren't trying their best to find a cure for them. Lots of doctors decided to be doctors after seeing bad stuff on the news about some horrible disease. Maybe you might want to become a doctor or a medical researcher someday so that one day you might find the cure for a terrible disease. Becoming a healer is a wonderful thing to do with your life. Just think of how many big diseases that used to kill people are no longer a huge threat to people in North America because some healer did a great thing with his or her life:

- Smallpox
- Polio
- Diphtheria
- Measles and German measles
- Mumps
- Rabies

Maybe you'll be the one to find the cure for AIDS or one of the other diseases that nobody can cure today. Maybe that's what you're supposed to do with your life. Maybe that's what God built you for. There are lots of ways you can use your life for good, but being a healer is one great way. If you stop thinking about diseases as cruel and unfair and start thinking of them as great puzzles to solve, then you can stop feeling so sad and get to work with other healers to make a difference in this world.

nd Boy Burned in Stunt Imit

Some Swiss, Aghast at Risks

Rules for 'Extreme Sports'

The Feuding Of Celebrities Is Old Ne

Reducing

Low Seat Belt Use Linked to

Passive Smoke Makes For Massive Risks

Hip-Hop Star Acqu
In Shooting

Night
Celebriti
the legal sp
ast they
lawyers

Snack Attack!
Kids are eating a lot more calories between
meals—and they have the bellies to prove it

12. BAD FOR THEM, GOOD FOR YOU?

When you see stuff on TV that upsets other people, but not you . . . when your clothes or music freak out your parents . . . when the bad stuff doesn't seem so bad to you.

We've been talking this whole time about bad stuff in the news as if everybody agrees on what bad stuff is. Everybody does agree that hunger and sickness and flooding and killing are really bad. But there are other things that make the headlines and that crop up in magazines and in TV shows that only *some* people think are bad.

More and more, we're seeing news headlines, talk shows, and radio stories about famous people and their private

109

lives—whether or not we want to hear about them. We definitely think it's bad news for the world to hear about the sad problems that often go along with being famous—ugly divorces, eating disorders, drug addiction, and lots of other bad stuff. But a lot of people, even kids, like to hear about the problems of the rich and famous because it makes normal people feel like their lives are better even though they aren't rich.

Sometimes certain types of music seem bad to some people and good to others. Adults pretty much always hate the music that their kids love—that's just part of life! Our parents hated rock and roll. Now that we're adults, we don't like rap music. And believe it or not, when you grow up and have kids, they'll probably think hip-hop is for old fogies!

Kids and grown-ups also usually disagree about clothing styles, too. Our parents hated things like sideburns, tight jeans, and slicked back hair that we thought looked great. We hate baggy clothes, underwear sticking out of pants, fluorescent hair, and baseball caps worn backward. Chances are that when you grow up and have kids of your own, you'll probably hate the music they listen to and the way they dress, too.

Body piercing and tattoos are not new, but it's pretty new to see them on people who aren't in motorcycle gangs. Seeing movie and music stars and kids with metal studs in their ears, belly buttons, tongues, and lips freaks out a lot of adults, but for kids who do it, it's just a cool way to decorate their bodies.

Often, a lot of celebrities who are loved by kids are hated by parents. TV stars, rock stars, and sports stars who look weird, get in trouble with the police, have drug problems, wear revealing clothes, or have kids with people they're not married to are hated by some and are heroes to others. A lot of kids idolize professional wrestlers. But some adults think that pro wrestling has too much violence and sex and that these wrestlers are just goony actors and a bad influence.

You've probably also heard your parents say that really thin girls on TV are a bad influence because they might make young girls develop eating disorders like anorexia. Anorexia is when a person is afraid to eat because she is afraid to gain weight, which can cause her to starve herself to death. No matter how thin anorexics are, they always feel fat. Adults worry that if their daughters see really thin girls on TV and in magazines all the time, they will make themselves sick trying to be beautiful. But the girls (and boys) don't see what the big deal is about looking at and admiring people they think are beautiful.

Probably one of the biggest things grown-ups are freaking out about these days are violent video games where there's a lot of killing and blood and guts splashing all over the screen. Some adults think that these video games might lead kids to act in violent ways. Kids just like to play the games to test their skills. They think they're cool. They say they know the difference between real killing and fake killing.

And speaking of killing, gangs are definitely bad stuff in

the news in rougher neighborhoods. But for the people who join them, gangs are families and friends and places where people respect you. In tough neighborhoods, joining a gang is seen as a way of being protected. So you see, it all depends on your experience and point of view.

STUFF TO UNDERSTAND

How can you tell if something is really a bad thing on TV or in the news if not everybody in your life agrees about it? This isn't always easy, but it's one big thing you're going to have to think about when you become a teenager.

One thing you can do is remember that lots of things that people say are bad are really just things that people think are ugly. Ugly is different than bad. Ugly is a measure of beauty and bad is a measure of right and wrong. These are two very different things and it's important not to get them mixed up. People have different ideas about what is beautiful (or not) and that's just fine. That's the way people are supposed to be. Beauty isn't about right or wrong.

Part of growing up is figuring out what kind of things are definitely right and what kinds of things are definitely wrong. Right and wrong are real and true, and they have nothing to do with what you want them to be. If there's no right and wrong that's absolutely positively true, then maybe Hitler was right when he murdered six million Jews, and maybe Stalin was right when he killed millions of Russians who opposed him. Maybe Mao Tse-tung was right when he killed so many Buddhist monks in Tibet. Maybe the Hutu tribe was right when they killed almost a million members of the Tutsi tribe in Rwanda in 1994.

> **Right and wrong are real and true, and they have nothing to do with what you want them to be.**

Some things are just completely, absolutely, no-question-about-it wrong, and when you see them you have to be able to say without any doubt: "That's terrible and disgusting and wrong." It's important to figure out which things those are. But how a kid wears his pants and what a kid sticks into her belly button and what color a kid dyes his hair isn't right or wrong. It's about what is beautiful, and that question has no final, true answer.

STUFF YOU CAN FIX

What are you supposed to do about things on the news your parents hate that you like or even love? One thing you can do is to try to see things from their side before you freak out. Even though your parents are older and probably "uncool," they love you and they want the best for you. It's a good thing to try to get your folks to understand why you like the music you like, and it's also good to try to understand why they like the music they like. Broadening your musical interests is good for everybody. If you want your folks to try to understand you, it seems fair to us that you ought to try just as hard to understand them. A lot of unhappiness in this world could be avoided if parents and kids talked a little bit more and tried to understand each other a lot more.

> **If you want your folks to try to understand you, it seems fair that you ought to try just as hard to understand them.**

The "gray areas" of bad stuff—the stuff in life that isn't really clear or "black and white"—are not about fixing. They are about thinking, learning, studying, and exploring. Growing up is all about this: You start to figure out what's good for you and bad for you, what works for you and doesn't work for you, what's beautiful to you and ugly to you. You are growing a wonderful mind of your own, but that takes guidance from people who love you—friends and family and clergy and teachers—and it also takes mistakes. (We just hope that mistake won't be a permanent tattoo on your arm of some crazy monster that your grandchildren will have to look at when you're baby-sitting them fifty years from now!)

Over many years, the really good and the really beautiful things in our world last. We can all wait to know what turns out to be really beautiful, but we can't wait to know what is right and what is wrong. Everything depends on that.

13. LIFE ISN'T PERFECT YET

When you finally understand that life isn't perfect and that this is perfectly okay.

Life just isn't perfect yet. That's the most simple and most important idea in this book. We need to remember this so that we keep trying to fix the broken parts in the world and in ourselves. Our responsibility is never to stop trying to make the world better and to make ourselves better. But we can't get depressed just because we're too small, or too young, or too powerless, or too broken to make the world completely perfect right now. It's the trying that matters most.

And even though trying to fix the world means that we will lose sometimes, losing is a better thing than you might realize. Most of the people who always get what they want and never lose are really not that nice. They don't understand that the world will not always bow down to them. Losing gives us character. Losing makes us stronger because it makes us try to do even better the next time. Remember,

Michael Jordan didn't make his high school basketball team the first time he tried out! Albert Einstein flunked math, and Abraham Lincoln went bankrupt in some businesses before he became president. Losing can be as big a part of growing as winning.

Death is also a challenge that can help us grow. We can learn how to help those who have just lost a dear one. We can try to end the hunger or disease or poverty that caused the death. We can learn that death may end life, but death can never end hope. Hope is what keeps us alive. We hope that tomorrow will be better than today. And we work for that day with all our heart and all our might and all our soul.

Religious people say that a person called the Messiah will bring the news of that day when the world will at last be perfect. Christians call that Messiah Jesus Christ. Jews and Muslims have different names but the same hope. The main thing is that we're all a part of this world and its story of suffering. But we're also a part of overcoming that suffering. Maybe in our lifetime, or maybe in yours, or maybe in the lifetime of the children of your children's children, there will come a day when justice really will flow like a river and kindness will be like a well that never runs dry. Please work and pray for that day when there will be no more bad stuff in the news.

God bless us one and all!